Writing Romance

Writing Romance

The Ultimate Guide on Craft, Creation and

Industry Connections

Written by the members of the
San Francisco Area Romance Writers of America, and guests

SFA-RWA Publishing

WRITING ROMANCE
THE ULTIMATE GUIDE ON CRAFT, CREATION AND INDUSTRY CONNECTIONS

SFA-RWA Publishing
771 Kingston Ave., #108
Piedmont, CA 94611
sfarwabook2008@gmail.com

Printed in the United States of America

Library of Congress cataloging-in-Publication Data has been applied for.

ISBN #: 978-0-615-20261-7

Cover design by Josie Brown and Jane George
Book Design by Beth Barany and Jane George
Edited by Beth Barany, Shelley Bates, Kay Keppler, Karen Morison-Knox

SFA-RWA Publishing books are available for special promotions and premiums. Please contact us for details.

Acknowledgments

Thank you to all who made this book possible: Beth Barany, Shelly Bates, Josie Brown, Elizabeth Edwards, Tonda Fuller, Jane George, Kay Keppler, Shannon Monroe, Carol Lynn Simpson, Karen Morison-Knox, Monica Newcomb, Karin Ohlson, Patricia Simpson, Regan Taylor, and Poppy Southcott who suggested we do this back in Dallas in 2004, and Cathy Yardley, the then chapter president, who agreed.

CONTENTS

PART II: CRAFT

Part III: Connection

PREFACE

by Karin Tabke,
San Francisco Area Romance Writers of America (SFA-RWA)
chapter president, 2007-2008

"I can write a romance novel."

I can't tell you the number of times someone has said that to me. Usually it happens after I've toiled three months straight, practically 24/7, on my latest novel. I think for all those sleepless nights I've stayed up until three o'clock in the morning, adding nuance to my heroine's personality, striving to make a love scene jump off a page, hoping that my readers will fall in love with my hero, as I have.

Which is why my answer to them—and to you, too—is: "Bring it on."

And I mean it. If you're serious about giving it your best shot, you'll need to read every page of this book. Its contributors, mostly published authors and book industry professionals, know what it takes to create a romance novel, from a kernel of an idea to bestseller.

Trust me, this book will be your bible. From it you'll create your career mandate. And with the knowledge gleaned from its pages, you'll accomplish your dream:

To write the next great romance novel, with characters that make us laugh, cry, and fall in love with them.

Then, when we do run into each other, you won't say, "I can write a romance novel" but "I've just sold a romance novel!"

And I'll answer, "Welcome to the club."

INTRODUCTION
By Beth Barany, Project Coordinator

Many aspects go into writing a romance novel. The creative process, the craft of writing, and last but not least, the industry connections needed to get our work published and on bookstore shelves or on a website. Our contributors have touched on each of these topics in the three sections: Creation, Craft, and Connections.

So, where do we begin? Why simply at the beginning. You can read this anthology straight through, or jump around, reading the articles that speak to you. I guarantee you will find useful information on every page. Some of you may be reading this information for the first time, and we hope that it will stimulate you to reach for the next book and the next class on that topic, and encourage you to start your first novel. For those of you for whom this information is review, I invite you to let it propel you back to your manuscript and toward story completion.

There is nothing we writers like more than a great read. The writers of the San Francisco Romance Writers of America (RWA) chapter, and valued outside contributors, have worked hard to give you that here, in bite-sized pieces, so enjoy.

And be sure to check out our Featured Author Profiles in the back, along with the Ultimate Resource for Writing Romance: a listing of RWA chapters, and the agents and publishers accepting romance.

Lastly, check out our sponsors, romance-friendly vendors, without whom this anthology would not have seen the light. We thank you!

Be inspired, get writing, get published!

PART I

CREATION

"To really tell a story, I need to write it. It's then that I understand what it is that I'm really trying to say. I find deeper meaning—and the deeper satisfaction."

-- *Escaping into the Open: the Art of Writing True* by Elizabeth Berg

You are a Wellspring of Creativity
By Beth Barany

Call it free writing, splash writing, flash writing, brain dumping, brain mapping, brainstorming, warming up, or letting it all hang out. It doesn't matter what you call it. What matters is that it—this act of preparation—works for any kind of artist. It frees up the mind and the hand and prepares you for the work ahead.

The act of free writing or sketching generates ideas, emotions, thoughts, feelings, and images that tug at your heart and rouse you to laugh, cry, shout, or sing. And to envision. Though you may not know why you need to write or what your thoughts will morph into, as a first step, it is the act of writing that is important.

The power of this kind of fast-and-loose work generates a positive yes in your mind and soul. Here's how it works.

Name the unnamable.
Free writing, free-form movement, and doodling says yes to your subconscious and yes to pouring forth and naming what was before unnamable—primarily your feelings, fears, hopes, dreams, and mental pictures—so you can name, examine, share, and release them.

Let the well overflow.
Free-form creating says yes to your infinite wellspring of creativity because every time—and I mean every time—that you say yes to it by writing down a line, word, or phrase, you're telling your subconscious to send you more. The more you allow your creative ideas to flow, and the more you act on the creative thoughts and images by recording them as they arrive, the more they will zoom into your mind, pouring out of you like a crashing waterfall at high spring, fat with the snowmelt.

Free up brain space.
Contrary to the fear that you're wasting your time, your freedom at the flash-creation stage releases the static of worry. Because you're clearing out the debris in the closet of your mind, you can hear your intuition and creative mind whenever it shows up.

Take care of your Self.
Free-form creating, whether on the page or in three dimensions, feels good. Otherwise, why do it? Besides that, it's fun! It's part of the care and feeding of your soul. You are taking care of yourself. Congratulations!

Based in Northern California, Beth Barany is working on a young adult adventure fantasy series about Henrietta, the Dragon Slayer. She's also a workshop leader, book coach and creativity consultant for writers, artists, business professionals and entrepreneurs. For her e-book, *Overcome Writer's Block: 10 Writing Sparks to Ignite Your Creativity*, and other writing support, see www.overcomewritersblock.com.

The Writer's GMC
By Tawny Weber

We've all heard how important they are . . . goal, motivation, and conflict. Undeniably some of the most powerful tools in the writer's toolbox. As many beginning writers have heard—especially if they spend any time on the contest circuit—GMC is the glue that holds a plot together. It's the magic that breathes life into our characters, into our story. But did you know they are just as important to us personally, as we carefully hone our writing careers?

Goals
I'm sure there are great writers who've been published without ever setting goals. Others who've had great success with the simple goal of "get published." For most of us, however, working with goals is an important part of our process of moving from beginner to contest winner to that pivotal goal turning point, contracted author. How do we learn to use goals to our advantage? There are plenty of fabulous goal workshops out there, plus articles and books devoted to the art of setting goals. There are even entire sections of the bookstore devoted to helping us figure it out.

But the bottom line, for me, is what's the big picture? What do I want, and when do I want it? Before I sold, that goal was easy: to sell! Of course, I'd fleshed it out a little more. I knew I wanted to write for Harlequin, and that my voice and writing style best fit Blaze. I pursued the goal through contests, studying the books put out by that line, and working revisions, so when I did sell to Harlequin Blaze, it was definitely a hard-earned goal.

Once that initial goal to sell is met, what next? A new goal. Each published author's goals will be a little different, of course, but there are common threads: more sales, hitting lists, making money.

Motivation
Once the new goals are in place, it's time to bring on our next element: motivation. Just as there are writers who've succeeded without goals, there are many who've made it without worrying about staying motivated. Somehow, they have an inner fire that constantly fuels them. For the rest of us, the motivation to face that blank page or muddled mess of edits each day is only slightly less intimidating than parading naked through the grocery store.

So, how can we stay motivated? What gets us through the long, lonely hours of ripping our soul apart to find the words that will do justice to the pictures dancing in our heads? Like our characters, we all have different motivations. The trick is finding them.

A quick search through my own motivational toolbox turns up a few things that have worked well for me. One of the strongest is a support team, a group to sound off to. Writers who will encourage or commiserate, who really understand the voices in my head as well as the ups and downs of this industry. You might find your support group at your local or online RWA chapter. Plotting groups and other writing groups are great sources of support as well. Critique groups and writing partners are one of the strongest means of support and motivation, since they often know your work as well as you do. Contests offer further validation, although the discouragement can sometimes outweigh the motivation. Another tool I'm fond of is books—go figure. The self-help aisle at the bookstore is teeming with books on motivation, time management, improving self-esteem, and personal growth.

Conflict

What was that last one? Conflict?

Yeah, like we need ideas on bringing conflict into our writing lives. Aren't lack of time, unreliable Muses, real-life demands and tragedies, and those ever-so-derailing rejections enough? I'd say if there is one area we're amply equipped in, it's conflict. The trick is learning to overcome it, to use it, or simply to work around it. Impossible, you say? Nope, just challenging. I've written through family tragedy, around holidays, and learned to compensate for my lifelong procrastination habit. I'm even working hard to overcome my inability to say no when asked to volunteer!

One tool that helps in the face of conflict is a solid writing habit—that ingrained process of putting your butt in the chair and your fingers on the keyboard. Every writer uses a different process, has a different habit, but the key for all the authors I've talked to is to Just Do It. Write. Once you figure out what your process is, maximize it. Use it. It's that writing habit that will see many an author through the face of conflict.

Other than habit, what's the true key to keeping conflict from messing up our writing career's Happily Ever After? It all comes back to the right goal and the right motivation. If the goal is one that you are passionate about, one that you believe in—you're willing to fight for it. If you have the motivational resources to fall back on in the face of conflict, you'll weather whatever storms life tosses at you and achieve your goals and that Happily Ever After.

Just as your manuscript needs GMC, so does your writing career. The true key, of course, is finding yours.

Three-time Golden Heart finalist Tawny Weber dreams up stories in her California home, surrounded by dogs, cats, and kids. Her next book, *Risque Business*, is a September 2008 Harlequin Blaze release. She loves to hear from readers—visit her at www.TawnyWeber.com.

The Writer's GMC Worksheet:
Know What You Want
By Beth Barany

You have a dream! You want to write a book. Congratulations! Happy dance! So now what? How do you go from great idea to great reality? With The Writer's GMC, that's how. Answer the questions below to uncover your writing goals, motivations, and conflicts. You can do it! This next step requires your handy tools of creativity, honesty, and perseverance.

G is for Goal

What is your current writing project? What are your long-term writing projects? Describe each one in as much detail as possible, addressing, for example, genre, length, and audience.

M is for Motivation

What is the main motivation fueling you—to write in general and to work on your current project? What are your secondary motivations? Dig deep and be honest with yourself. Some write because their day isn't complete without it; others write to communicate a message or a dream, make a point, or impress others. There is no wrong answer—only clarity achieved by knowing why you write.

C is for Conflict

Focus on your perceived obstacles, both internal and external. Recognize any negative or limiting self-talk for what it is—an obstacle to be overcome. Notice what external factors interrupt the path to your writing time: busyness, work and family obligations, or TV watching. No judgment here. Only notice that these obstacles are often there by our own choosing and that by recognizing them we can choose differently. We can find solutions through our strengths. What strengths, both internal and external, can you use to achieve your writing goals? Include inner qualities like humor, intelligence, curiosity, and drive, and outer benefits such as a space to work, a regular schedule that allows for writing, a nice computer, or no pressure to make money at your writing.

Share

Congratulations! Now that you are clarifying your writing goals, motivations, conflicts, and strengths, share them with a supportive writing buddy, writers' group, teacher, or coach. By sharing your GMC, you up the ante for yourself. You are responsible for your own goals, and sharing helps you stay accountable for your stated goals. Also, a success buddy can cheer you on and validate that action you took toward your dream today. Lastly, a buddy or writing group, coach, or teacher can encourage you to plan and execute your next step.

Next Step

So what is the next step in your writing project? Do you need to sit down and write? Do you need support to review and activate your GMC? Do you need to create a project timeline? Lastly, what support, kudos, and rewards will you need along the way? Don't forget those. None of us achieves a dream without many people helping us. Welcome to the Writers Community of the World!

*Thanks to Deb Dixon and her book, *Goal, Motivation and Conflict*, for inspiration for this article. See Gryphon Books for Writers for more information.

 Based in Northern California, Beth Barany is working on a young adult adventure fantasy series about Henrietta, the Dragon Slayer. She's also a workshop leader, book coach and creativity consultant for writers, artists, business professionals and entrepreneurs. For her e-book on overcoming writer's block, check out www.overcomewritersblock.com.

Here, Story, Story, Story...

By Jane George

Stories, with a capital S, are the fibrous strands that unite all human experience. From childhood, when our strongest memories become mythologized, we look for connections between our personal legends and our world. Stories give us these connections. Plot and character, then, are the twigs and bits of fluff used by authors to construct our story nests, the places where we writers grow, rest, build, and fly from.

Writers are tireless collectors of story-building materials. A keen observer will be able to feather her story with a fine collection of the pithy tidbits of human interaction. A keen observer's mind overflows with raw material. Where do all of these raw building materials coalesce? In dreams.

My strongest stories have all come to me in my dreams. Often, not the entire plot arc, but a complete, fleshed-out scene with incredible impact will play itself out before I wake. These scenes tend to be so powerful that they're impossible to forget. I'm forced to write them down.

I'm an advocate of keeping dream journals—or at least a pad of paper on the nightstand. I've lost many a "brilliant" conversation between characters because I failed to write it down upon waking. Twilight time, that space between sleep and wakefulness, is precious for story building.

A good way to become a keen observer, if you're not one already, is to give yourself the gift of enforced solitude. Go places alone. I don't mean an isolated beach; all that will inspire you to write is Jonathan Livingston Seagull. I mean go people-watching, to cafés, to PTA meetings (sit in the back or you'll end up volunteering, not writing). Ride buses. Start a sketchbook. Even if you aren't artistically gifted, forcing yourself to sit and draw, to truly look, will make you a better observer. And being quiet makes for better eavesdropping—er, listening. Soon, even those day-job office meetings become ripe with potential material. Well, perhaps not, but writing, like painting, is a way of observing our world.

By placing our private observations within the larger framework of Story, we get to change our worlds, and those of our readers, by stretching the wings of our creativity. Looking for a story idea? Look more closely.

Jane George writes paranormal historical romance and mainstream black comedy. She lives in the San Francisco area's East Bay, on the sunny side of the fog line.

Facing the Blank Page
By Shannon L. Monroe

I may die before I learn the craft of writing on the computer. There is just something unnatural to me about staring at a cursor or an empty Word document. The ideas do not flow as they should. My pleasure comes from writing with an incredibly expensive pen on a really cheap Mead® composition notebook. I know this may not be the way most writers go about their novels, but it is what works for me. I love the search for a quality, top-notch fine point and the crackle of the brand new binding on the notebook.

I struggle with getting started. I will go for days staring at the blank first page, wondering what it is that will trigger the stories, the characters, and make them come alive. I have been writing for more than 20 years, but I still go through the same downtime and then I get an epiphany, the same way each time.

My muse is music.

I get all my inspiration and passion for writing from listening to music: in my car, in my headphones, in a movie theater—it doesn't matter. But the real spark for me is seeing live music. Attending a concert, I can come up with at least five scenes, plots, dark moments, sex scenarios, anything to do with my new or in-progress romance.

If you haven't tried it, I highly recommend giving a concert a go. There are hordes of people in every shape, size, height, race, and form of dress to observe. There are a million things happening or that could happen—situations you could insert your characters into. I listen to what the musicians are creating on stage and feel all the intimate moments their lyrics bring alive inside of me.

Think about the way a favorite scene in a movie or television show stays with you. For me, it is always the song that was strategically placed there, right where it should be, that makes it stick. Remember the overhead, boom-box plea of John Cusack's Lloyd Dobler in Say Anything? Not to take anything away from the actors or the writing and directing of Cameron Crowe and his team, of course, but if Peter Gabriel's classic hit "In Your Eyes" hadn't been blasting away at that exact moment, something magical would have never come across to us as an audience.

If you get stuck for an idea or how to get started, even when your story or your characters are bursting to break free, listen to music. Preferably live music. And remember to take your pen and paper with you.

Shannon Monroe graduated from UC Berkeley with a degree in Ancient Greek and Roman History and resides in Oakland, California. Some of her pleasures include traveling, concerts, Austen, Homer, Salinger, Garwood, and Pearl Jam.

Getting Through a Blocked Point in Your Novel

By Judy Sabel Soifer

I've been told I have a gift for helping writers through that point in their story where they are stuck. But it would be an even greater gift if I could share it with all of you.

By the time they seek my help, the writers have already tried the usual methods, like reading through the last section they've written, putting it away for a while, or working on another part of the book. There are three key elements that help me help them: creativity, intuition, and patience. When authors contact me about being stuck, I either have them call me or meet me in person. Simply reading the manuscript isn't the same as hearing the story. You can't hear the writer's joys and frustrations when you read.

I ask writers to tell me about their stories first, then the part where they are stuck. This is where patience comes in. You have to really listen with all of your heart. When you do, your intuition will tell you what's wrong. Often it's not the scene they are stuck on, but something earlier in the plot, or the plot itself. By listening, you find something doesn't ring true or make sense. The author has been too close to see this, but as an outside listener, you're not. Usually talking things through will help the author see this.

The last part involves using your creativity—helping writers to find new ways to fix what's wrong. I am very creative, so I love doing this. It's a lot like a brainstorming session.

I know I'm not the only one who possesses all of these qualities. I've just figured out how to put them together to help others. Writers are creative, intuitive people. The patience part is just like reading a book, only someone is telling you about the book. Close your eyes and enjoy yourself. I'm sure you can help each other in the same way that I do. But if you ever find you're really stuck, I can be reached through the SFA-RWA chapter. Unless I start getting too many requests for help. I don't charge, so I only ask that you pay it forward.

Judy Sabel Soifer, writing as J.M. Sabel, is an ex-ballerina who hung up her dancing shoes to work with children in the field of nursing. She has a master's degree in pediatric nursing. She's a writer and illustrator working toward publication. Find out more about J.M Sabel and her books: web.mac.com/jmsabelsoifer

Battling Procrastination—One Day at a Time

By Sophie Littlefield

Procrastination isn't a vice unique to writers—but we sure are good at it. Consider how many people have been meaning to write a novel, have been working on the first chapter for months, or the first draft for years, or consistently find that their lives are too busy and their obligations too great to make any progress at all.

Now, consider whether this describes you.

It is entirely possible that writing doesn't matter to you as much as the other activities and duties that compete for your time. This is not a condemnation. If you consistently find yourself ranking writing below other obligations and activities, be honest with yourself about whether this is the right time in your life to write.

If, however, you want to make writing a high priority, but consistently let it slide, you need to change the way you approach the process. And to do so, you need to understand what is getting in your way.

For many of us, the biggest obstacle to our own success is fear. Fear dampens enthusiasm, cripples progress, and plagues many, many fine writers, both newcomers and veterans.

Before I understood the nature of my own fear about writing, I began to notice its physical manifestations. The thought of writing caused the same gut-tightening, pulse-quickening queasiness that I felt when I was about to speak in public or attend a cocktail party where I knew no one.

It didn't make sense to me. I was published in nonfiction. I had received a decent amount of praise and support for my work, and I believed I had a measure of raw talent and potential. I had several other advantages: a supportive husband, a terrific critique group, and a bit of free time every day that could be devoted to writing. I had no deficiency of story ideas, so "block" was not the problem.

One day I created an exercise for myself to try to understand where the fear was coming from. The exercise went like this:

I'm not afraid of writing, but if I were afraid, three possible reasons would be:

1. _____
2. _____
3. _____

The results stunned me. As soon as I gave myself permission to brainstorm, I wrote:

1. If I write, I might discover that I'm not any good at it.

25

2. If I write, I might find that I'm not as good at it as I used to be, and that all my previous success was sheer luck.

3. If I write, I'll have to take responsibility for reaching my own goals, and then I can no longer blame other people and factors for my lack of success.

These were not happy revelations. They did not suggest easy solutions. I wasted some more time resisting, and my output sank even further.

One day, I heard about a program where participants committed to writing one hundred words for one hundred consecutive days. You could write more if you liked, but you didn't have to. And the words didn't even have to be any good. I realized that this was a challenge I could meet. I wrote one hundred words, buoyed by the knowledge that they were allowed to be terrible. The next day I wrote a hundred more. I kept going, writing a few hundred words some days, sometimes even a thousand. I was working on a story I'd been dabbling at for an appalling four years. I took a deep breath and dug up notes so old they were rimed with dust. I hated every session, I believed in my soul I was writing dreck, but I kept going.

It got easier. Around day fifty it occurred to me that there ought to be something in this exercise for me, a little reward in case all I ended up with was 10,000 words of bad prose. I made my husband promise to take me out for a nice dinner when I got to 100. That did the trick. If I had a bad day, I'd just think, Oh well, that's going to be one hell of a nice dinner.

I also told my critique group what I was doing. I was surprised at how supportive they were. I resisted admitting that I was just writing junk.

One hundred days came and went. Dinner was fabulous. I ordered dessert—I deserved it. I came home and decided to see how much I'd written.

To my astonishment, I had written 87,000 words.

This was more than I'd written in the prior three years—and I'd done it in a little over three months.

I began this exercise exactly two years ago. Since then I've taken days off— once several weeks when my office was renovated—but I've never stopped. I've completed two manuscripts and begun a third. I've written articles, short stories, and book reviews, and I've become more careful and skilled at critiquing.

About eight months ago—253 days, to be exact—one of my dearest writing friends began a similar journey. Though she kindly gives me credit for inspiration, my belief is that she was ready on that day to conquer her own fears. She has an incredible book taking shape, a work that has us all cheering, a project worthy of her considerable skill and imagination.

Could it be your turn?

It's possible that fear is not your issue. But try the exercise anyway. Then make a deal with yourself.

For me, writing every day is critical. Days off don't work; they interrupt my flow and send me plummeting back to uncertainty. I've had to be creative, writing while sitting on a rock in Yosemite National Park; in the carpool line; in guest rooms; at family holidays; by the pool on vacation; and in subways, airplanes, and bathrooms.

Other writers report success with a variety of strategies. Some take weekends off, or count fifteen minutes of revising or line editing. The key is to make your goals very clear, and to be your own unyielding boss from hell. Not feeling well? Good thing it's only a hundred words. Desperate Housewives is almost on? Guess you'll miss the first fifteen minutes. Have absolutely nothing to say? Write about your frustration.

Naming your fears and creating a systematic approach to working around them is not easy. It won't turn you into Nora Roberts or Stephen King. It won't even cure your procrastination.

I will still do just about anything to avoid sitting down to the computer. My family has the cleanest, fluffiest, most beautifully pressed clothing in the neighborhood because I would much rather do laundry than work.

And yet, every day I eventually run out of excuses. I sit down, fears and all, and I work. I write a hundred words. Sometimes I write more. Sometimes I write so much and so well that I forget that I hate the process.

The fears are losing the battle. More and more, I entertain only doubts, fear's weak cousins. Working every day has shifted my self-identity; now, if anyone asks, I'll answer with conviction: I am a writer. Some days a fine one, other days an embattled one, but most definitely and permanently a writer.

Resource: Club100—a Yahoo!® Group, moderated by Beth Pattillo. Visit www.bethpattillo.com/id8.html.

Sophie Littlefield writes women's and crime fiction and has completed several manuscripts. Her short story "Anything for You" is a runner-up for the Crime Writers' Association's 2007 Fish-Knife Award.

The Fifteen-Minute Solution
Or, I'm a Single Mom with Children and a Full-Time Job (or Whatever). How Do I Go About Getting Time to Write?
By Carol Lynn Stewart

Time is a really bizarre thing, have you noticed? When you are waiting for something, time seems to sit right on your chest until the weight of it is almost unbearable, yet it slides effortlessly around you when you're engaged in doing something you love, such as making love or, well, writing about making love, and then there you are, looking at the clock, wondering how the hell hours slipped by without your awareness of their passing.

There are so many things in a writer's life that have a serious claim on the writer's attention. For me it was being a single mother. School lunches needed to be made; play time arranged; after-school programs, though I paid an arm and a leg for them, always required parent volunteer time; and my day job just never seemed to let up. Even lunch hours were consumed with completing projects. After I got home, dinner and homework were front and center, as well as all the delicious cuddling and sweet, silly games that are just a small slice of the enormous gift parenthood bestows. A bit of this, a chunk of that and suddenly it would be after nine, my child tucked into bed. Finally, there it was: A moment to write. I would sit my butt in my computer chair and stare at the blank page on the screen, cursor blinking. I knew that getting up at 5:00 a.m. would mean I had about half an hour, at most, to sink into my new story, write a few sentences, and then rip myself away from it.

Unfortunately, the page stayed blank for months. Many days found me beyond exhaustion and I often woke up with my cheek mashed onto my keyboard and random letters from my keyboard-diving face filled page after page of the text program. How could this happen? I'd already written a gargantuan paranormal medieval that was published soon after my divorce. On top of that, I'd reviewed books for ForeWord and never missed a deadline. So what was wrong? I went straight into despair until a friend from my graduate school days reminded me how I had researched, written, and edited my dissertation during the first two years of my child's life, while working thirty hours a week at my day job. "Remember the fifteen-minute solution?" she asked.

Oh, right! When I was writing my dissertation, clinical psychologist Joan Bolker had written an article on how to start, revise, and complete a dissertation. She later expanded this into a book, but the core of her article was how to create a writing discipline in the middle of an already overextended life. The essence of her article was to work in snippets of time. This gave the writer permission to write; it's only fifteen minutes a day, right? Who can't find fifteen minutes, even in the most overstuffed of schedules?

Soon, writing became a luxury. Once I allowed myself fifteen minutes a day to write, the floodgates opened and page after page poured out. If I scheduled the fifteen minutes right before I went to bed, I'd start at 9:30 and the next thing I knew it would be midnight. So I played with my fifteen-minute snippets. I found that by carrying around a small notebook, I could stick my writing time into any space where "waiting" happened, such as at the doctor's office or waiting for people to arrive for meetings.

If you find yourself overextended and blocked, please give this a try! It got at least ten women in my graduate cohort through the "not enough time to complete the thesis because (fill in the blank)" and writing romance is so much more engaging and fun than writing a dissertation.

Carol Lynn Stewart works at a major university in northern California. Her publishing credits include *Door In The Sky*, a medieval paranormal, with Hard Shell Word Factory, and "Angel Web," a contemporary Wiccan fantasy romance in *Words Of The Witches*, Berkley Jove. Visit her website at www.carolinamontague.com.

The Right Way to Write
By Candice Hern

I've spent fifteen years writing seriously—going to conferences and workshops, hanging out with other writers, and working with critique and brainstorming partners—and if there is one thing I've learned, it's that no two writers approach their work in exactly the same way.

I've been a detailed outliner from my very first book. Creating the outline can be an excruciating process, but I can't work without that roadmap. Some of my best friends are pantsers, that is, seat-of-the-pants writers. They make it up as they go and the idea of outlining makes their heads explode. Most pantsers feel they will lose the thrill of discovery by following an outline, whereas my acts of discovery happen in the creation of the outline. That doesn't mean I don't make small, unexpected discoveries along the way, but I find my story in the outlining process. Some pantsers are very linear, writing a first draft from beginning to end. Some are more random and episodic in their approach, writing scenes out of order as the muse strikes, and somehow putting them all together in a smooth and coherent end product. (Diana Gabaldon has said she writes this way, and there's no arguing with her success.) I know one writer who starts by writing the first love scene, even if it takes place on page 300, and then goes back to the beginning. Most outliners I know write one draft and we're done (because we've got an outline to guide us). Pantsers will sometimes write three, four, or ten drafts before they have a final product.

Whatever works, works.

The non-pantsers among us may use character charts, GMC (goal /motivation /conflict) charts, spreadsheets of scenes, backstory charts, maps of the twelve stages of the hero's journey, color-coded Post-It® notes, index cards, collages, whiteboards tracking story and character arcs, and notebooks stuffed to bursting with notes on story, character, research, and so on. Some of us—even some of us outliners—get intimidated by all that organization. But others may find one or more of these tools help to unleash their stories in the best possible way. Whatever works, works.

Productivity is also part of the process. Some people write ten pages a day every day. Some write twenty, or more. Some are lucky to finish five good pages in a week. Some writers allow themselves to write crap, so long as they write, and will revise it later. My friend Kate Moore used to have a sign on her computer that said, "Write bad sentences." Meaning: Write something. Anything. Just write. Others have to polish each sentence before moving to the next one. How much and how fast we produce is as individual as the rest of the writing process.

The point is that no one process is The Right Way. If it works for you, it's right. Don't worry about how someone else writes her book. Don't allow yourself to feel like a fraud because you think you're doing it The Wrong Way. If you try to force yourself to work like your critique partner, who exclaims about the benefits of her wall full of story charts, you may find that her process doesn't work for you and in fact creates a level of self-doubt that makes it impossible to write at all. Trying to use those story maps or color-coded Post-It® notes when all they do is confuse you is only going to bring you to a grinding halt. You may spend too much time worrying over the process when what you really should be doing is writing.

The process, your process, will find you in the writing. Suddenly you may realize that you can never get past chapter three without a character backstory chart, so creating that chart before you get to chapter three becomes part of your process. Or you realize that your first chapter always takes ten times as long to write as the next twenty chapters, so you build that time into your schedule. Or maybe whenever you reach page 200 it always seems that what you've written is totally unpublishable crap that will be the death of your career and you want to trash the whole thing and start over. We all (except maybe Nora) have our moments of angst with each book, but even those moments are often part of the predictable pattern of our work, so just accept it as your process. You know you will get through it. You always do.

And don't let the staggering productivity of your friends or colleagues make you feel guilty or unworthy. Some of us simply work more slowly than others, and you just have to accept that about yourself, that your process is a slow one. Allison Brennan can write a complete book in six weeks. I can barely do six chapters in six weeks. But worrying over Allison's productivity and success will not make me write any faster. In fact, it slows me down even more, just thinking about it!

No one can make up the rules for someone else. Make your own rules by finding what works for you. Experiment with all the tricks and tools you learn about in workshops. Try everything, if you're so inclined, but keep only what works. Not all of it, or even most of it, will work.

Process is a very individual thing, almost a part of our internal wiring. For example, I am super-organized in most aspects of my life, with spreadsheets tracking everything from tax deductions to subsidiary rights royalties to Christmas card lists, so it is no surprise that I'm an outliner in my writing. It's just another manifestation of my anal personality. I could not "fly into the mist," as Jo Beverley calls it, to save my life, so I don't even try. I would blow a fuse in my wiring!

It may take some trial and error over a couple of books to find your process, but once you find it, don't let anyone mess with it! You know it works for you, so don't second-guess yourself. Trust in your process, embrace it, and protect it. For you, it is The Right Way.

Candice Hern is an award-winning author of 14 historical romances. Her books have won praise for their "intelligence and elegant romantic sensibility" (*Romantic Times*) as well as their "delicious wit and luscious sensuality" (*Booklist*). Her latest book is the third in her award-winning Merry Widows trilogy, *Lady Be Bad*.

Tried and Convicted: A Prosecutorial Take on the Writer's Journey

By Virna DePaul

What do criminal prosecutors and romance writers have in common? First, neither can control their "wins." While talent, preparation, passion, and integrity help, they don't ensure a guilty verdict or publication. Second, many stages of criminal procedure mirror the writer's journey.

Writers get detained when fear stalls their forward momentum. Don't wait for perfection, that critical class, or a complete plot. Revise, learn, and be inspired along the way. Be arrested by your passion. Write despite busy schedules and insecurities. Give up TV and wake up at two a.m. if you have to.

At arraignment, defendants plead guilty or not guilty. Writers also make choices. Write every day and seek support from RWA and local chapters. Occasionally, break with conventional wisdom. Pitch an unfinished manuscript (but be honest about it) and bring some pages with you. Someone might read them.

A writer's preliminary hearing is when she lets her critique partner, a contest judge, or an agent or editor read her writing for the first time. Don't hide your writing away. Submit requested material. Enter contests (just be prepared for contradictory comments). Prove your case by writing to be read.

Critics try to suppress a writer's words. Whose advice do you take? Consider constructive criticism, but don't eliminate "you" from your writing. Make a well-reasoned decision and take responsibility for it.

The writer's trial is to tell the best story she can. Your goal is always to get to The End, then revise, polish, and perfect your closing argument (your pitch).

A writer's work will always be judged—with luck, by a lot more than 12 people. Verdicts don't always make sense. An editor may love your voice and plot, but not buy your book. Or you might make that elusive first sale, only to get panned by reviewers.

Have conviction in your goal and be proud that you wrote the best book possible.

Best of luck on your journey. I hope to see you along the way.

 Virna DePaul has been a criminal prosecutor since 1995. Her first manuscript placed second in the 2007 Smokey Mountain Laurie's single title category and landed Virna her dream agent, Kimberly Whalen. Virna's second manuscript, *Trial By Fury*, is about a female ex-SWAT sniper who must rely on a scarred ex-felon wrongly convicted of murder to save a little girl. For updates, criminal procedure information, or information on creating compelling heroes, visit Virna at http://chasingheroes.com or http://virnadepaul.com. Or, contact her via email at virna@chasingheroes.com.

Of Muppets and Men:
Writing Books, Raising Kids, Staying Sane
By Veronica Wolff

How do you find time to write when you have small children underfoot? The answer is simple: Daycare.

Done laughing yet? Good—it's either that or cry for those of us who can't afford nannies and au pairs. I live in the city and with sitters running $15 an hour, a simple dinner and movie becomes a three-figure affair. Now, if guilt were currency, I'd have enough left over to swing for daytime childcare, but sadly it's not and I don't.

I finished my first book when my son was three and my daughter was four, and friends have asked how I did it and stayed sane at the same time. While the jury's out on the whole sanity thing, I will share here a little of what did get me through those pages.

Let's get one thing straight from the outset. I'm not one of those women that other women envy. One of those how-does-she-do-it types with the impeccably clean house and the homemade treats for every PTA meeting. I confess I'm much more of a the-kids-are-finally-asleep-and-if-I-drink-my-glass-of-wine-in-the-living-room-I-won't-even-see-the-dinner-dishes-stacked-two-loads-deep-on-the-counter kinda gal.

I could say my secret weapon was television, and believe me, I've relied on my share of children's programming. But too long and I see their little eyes grow dim as their little brains begin to flat-line in front of the screen. Not to mention the fact that they do have a sixth sense about just when Mommy is beginning to jam on her book, don't they? Which, in our house, was always a don't-miss opportunity to fight viciously over something as precious as junk mail, or put gum in their sister's hair, or microwave a cell phone, or some other cataclysmic affair that put a full stop to the writing.

And besides, I need total silence to write. I vividly remember the day I wrote my very first love scene. I was grappling over just how to describe it— hmm, does she feel more of a rush or a wave?—and then I heard it. The clear, shrill, and unmistakable voice of Elmo announcing that, yes, he loves me. That sure put an end to my writing for the day.

So what did work, you ask? Unfortunately, the rest of my family lives far away, but I worked hard to cobble together a support community of people around me. If you look at the acknowledgments in my first book, you'll find almost a dozen names of folks who got me through, giving me the gift of time to write.

Don't get me wrong. You don't need a whole fleet of new best friends. I

35

found a wonderful mother's group in my neighborhood where I met some trustworthy and likeminded souls, and we formed our own childcare co-op. Among us was a yoga teacher, a musician, an artist . . . all people who needed whatever time they could grab to pursue their dreams. We were five families, each responsible for one morning a week, providing the food and paying the college student we'd found to assist. It's amazing what you can accomplish with a three-hour block of time in the remaining few mornings a week. Voila! Affordable daycare.

A mother's life is a series of fifteen-minute windows. You know what I mean. You put them in the swing, or put them down for a nap, or plop them in the sandbox and that timer begins ticking out its cruelly short span. You've got a limited chunk of time in which you can do a load of dishes, or fold laundry, or just stare into space, savoring the peace until the imminent next wave of kid-need. But surely it's not enough time in which to actually write, right?

Think again. With the right gear, you can get a lot done in those short, small windows of time. The AlphaSmart™ is a cheap and easy way to churn out pages in just those sorts of miniscule windows. How many times have you sat in your driveway staring into space, enjoying the silence of your children who decided two minutes from home that they were going to nap in the back seat instead of their crib, which by the way, they won't transfer to anyway? Those minutes add up. My page count spiked once I took to carrying my AlphaSmart™ in my diaper bag. It turns on with the flick of a button, and that flashing cursor beckons.

Then, once I signed my contract, I upgraded to a Mac notebook. It's faster than any PC, wakes and sleeps in the blink of an eye, and allowed me to add a paragraph here and there in one of my many stolen moments. Just don't forget every writer's analog weapon of choice: the notepad. I've got small ones in my car, my purse, my coat . . . I've even been known to write the odd thought on my hand. Inspiration can strike any time, and you need to be ready to jot it all down at the red light in the midst of your Thursday carpool.

Finally, carve out a space for yourself and build a hard-and-fast routine around it. Some writers work well in coffee shops. I'm a homebody myself, and have created my own home office. Sounds highfalutin', I know, so I'll be honest and tell you, I had my husband toss out dozens of old company logo T-shirts, found a small table at Ikea, and jammed it into a closet I now share with his clothes and all of our shoes. Fragrant? Perhaps. But mine, all mine.

The time you set aside for yourself is sacrosanct, so lower your bar and get used to an imperfect household. You know how it goes: you do the dishes, put in a load of laundry, and somehow two hours have evaporated. You'd never tell your boss you needed to go home to vacuum your daughter's room, or that you had to miss a meeting to put the clothes in the dryer. Don't do it to your other boss, that fabulous book of yours.

As I write this, my daughter is in first grade and my son in preschool, and the moment I walk into the house after dropping them off, I head straight for my sacred space. I don't succumb to the dishes, no matter how disgusting. I don't

Swiffer® up all those dog- and cat-fur tumbleweeds. I step gingerly over the pile of Lego® blocks, go straight to my "office," and put my bottom in that chair.

All those piles will wait, so don't fragment your time by ordering and reordering a home that the kids will turn around and mess up again anyway. Just blast some kid-friendly music at the end of the day and you'll have the place back in shape in no time—maybe even with your kids' help.

And if you have other responsibilities during the day, then take one hour before everyone else rises in the morning, or just after the kids are tucked in at night. It doesn't sound like much, but if you cut out the interruptions, all the web surfing and kitchen counter wiping, you'll be amazed at what you can accomplish.

Respect yourself and your work and treat writing like the job it is, even if you don't have a contract. Even if your book is still just a germ of an idea. I imagine—and am inspired by the fact that—there was a moment when even Nora herself had small kids underfoot and was contemplating that very first chapter.

Do as I say and not as I do with this last bit of wisdom. Taking time for a brisk walk or a gym visit will make you a better mom and a better writer both. Whether it's taking advantage of the soporific effects of a stroller or your local gym's child care, just thirty minutes will get those juices flowing and make you feel as if you've managed to carve out some time just for you.

Just be sure to have that notepad handy. You never know what you'll think of . . .

Veronica Wolff's heroines travel back in time to seventeenth-century Scotland, where they meet real heroes from history. Her second book, *Sword of the Highlands*, will be released in June 2008. Her kids don't understand why she's still not done writing her books.

Lunch with the Ladies or, How to Learn the Ins and Outs of the Writing Biz with Your Mouth Full
by Bella Andre

At least once a month, I have lunch with some of my favorite people in the world: other authors. These lunches are without question one of my favorite things to do. I'll squeeze the rest of my life around a get-together with the girls. Some are *New York Times* and *USA Today* bestsellers and some are just having their first romances published. But it's always a good time. And I always learn something about the business, about my writing, and, yes, even about myself. I've helped brainstorm plots and been given amazing help of every kind. Apart from writing great books, I'm not sure anything else is as important as the bonds we make with other writers.

Often, when I meet aspiring writers, they ask me, "How do you have the discipline to write every day?" The answer is twofold. Contract deadlines are an awfully good motivation, of course. But even more than that, I rely on my writing friends to help me to the finish line. One day in particular stands out in my mind.

I'd dropped off my kids by 10:00 a.m., which meant I had seven hours to make the 20-page goal I'd set for myself. Surprise, surprise, the hours slipped away. Cleaning the house, grocery shopping, packing for an upcoming vacation . . . the next thing I knew, I looked at the clock and it was 2:00 p.m. Only three hours left to write 20 pages before picking up the kids.

All I can say is, thank God for my network of writing friends. I sent out the following email to several of the usual suspects: "Help! I need to write 20 pages before 5:00 p.m. and somehow I've whittled away half the day. Can anyone meet me at Starbucks for a heads-down writing session?"

Within thirty seconds, the wonderful Anne Mallory wrote back. "I'll be there in five minutes." By the time she arrived, I was at our usual table, typing as fast as I could. We didn't speak much that day (some days are chattier than others, believe me), but I did learn that she'd also wasted most of the day on errands and was glad for the writing invite.

Eighteen pages later, before heading off to pick up my kids, I saved my work, shut down my computer, and promised to dedicate the book to Anne.

And that's why my best piece of writing advice is to encourage you to find a group of writers you can eat with, drink coffee with, and maybe even—on a really crazy day—crank out a stack of pages with.

Bella Andre would like to give public thanks to Jami Alden, Monica McCarty, Anne Mallory, Barbara Freethy, Candice Hern, and Carol Culver for all the hand-holding, butt-kicking, and plotting that went into her Bad Boys of Football series (Pocket Books, forthcoming in summer 2008) and her Hotshots: Men of Fire romantic suspense trilogy (Bantam Dell, forthcoming). For more information, please visit Bella's site at www.BellaAndre.com and check out her blogs with the Fog City Divas at www.fogcitydivas.typepad.com to meet some of her favorite lunch partners.

Finding Inspiration in Unlikely Places
By Jacqueline Harmon Butler

Inspiration for stories comes from the most unexpected places. You imagine you'll come up with ideas while walking in the woods, wading along the seashore, listening to beautiful music, or looking out at the view from the window of your study. Sure, all these situations are where one would expect enlightenment to show up. But for me, inspiration comes at the oddest times in the strangest places.

For example, I had just arrived at my boyfriend Claudio's home in Italy a few years ago to hear shocking news. His "other" girlfriend was pregnant, and that very afternoon her parents had kicked her out of the house and she had no place to go except Claudio's. It all seemed like a bad dream. And because I was planning on spending a week with him, I hadn't made arrangements for a hotel. It was already evening when I arrived, so I agreed to stay the night. I tossed and turned in the master bedroom at the top of the house while Claudio and the other girlfriend slept in the twin beds one floor below.

It wasn't one of my favorite memories. However, the next morning, in a fit of inspiration and frustration, I began to rework my novel, *Sono Claudio.* I had already decided to change it from a memoir to a fictional story and with the new situation, my imagination caught fire. I spent the entire day writing and plotting and drafting the story all the way to the end. Yes, I used the pregnant girlfriend bit, but from there on, the story was fictional. I turned the other girlfriend into a lying, venomous bitch that would stop at nothing to trap Claudio into a relationship with her.

Another unlikely muse appeared a year or so ago when I was lying on a gurney in the emergency room, so dizzy I couldn't walk. Countless medical people swirled around, poking at me and asking questions. While they waited for my lab tests to be completed, they moved on to other emergency patients and left me alone.

You can imagine I was scared. I thought I might be dying—I certainly felt like I was. My usual meditations and methods of relaxing weren't working, so in desperation, I thought of an idea for a new novel, and I started plotting the story as I lay on the gurney.

I decided that my heroine—I named her Julie Taylor—would be dying of a rare disease and be given six months to live. The more I thought about Julie and her story, the more I relaxed. Making up Julie's illness and problems and figuring out what she was going to do took my mind off my own situation.

As medical people passed, I told them I was working on a new novel and asked them questions about Julie's possible illness. What kind of disease might she have that would be deadly, but wouldn't incapacitate her? She shouldn't have any physical signs of her illness and be able to function normally while her ailment was slowly killing her. The concept ignited as we talked about all sorts of exciting topics like pancreatic cancer and leukemia. One of my doctors referred to pancreatic cancer as "peek and shriek" because that's what happens when they open someone up and find that type of cancer. It is quick and deadly. But I wanted something that could be healed magically or misdiagnosed or just go away to provide more freedom with my plot.

The medical staff was captivated by my constant questions. It got so that staff members would stop by every so often to hear more about the story.

On another occasion, when I had insomnia and my usual getting-to-sleep aids weren't working, I tried using what had always been a foolproof way to doze off. I imagined I was in Venice, and I was walking from the apartment where I usually stay near the Campo San Giacomo dell'Orio to the Piazza San Marco. I visualized the entire walk, all the little bridges, all the restaurants and houses. I checked out the wares in all the shop windows. I pictured myself in front of my favorite antique jewelry store. The shop keeps the lights on all night to illuminate the windows where the collections are displayed by stone: rubies in one tray, sapphires in another, emeralds and diamonds and pearls in yet others. I always like to play a game with myself: If I could choose one of the trays, which one would it be? The only rule was that I could select just one tray, and all the jewels on that tray. But even the total concentration of remembering each treasure in the collection didn't put me to sleep. I was getting nervous because I was almost to the Piazza San Marco and I was still wide awake.

In desperation, I imagined a totally new shop, one I had never seen before. Although it was late at night, the lights were still on, shining on exquisite silk garments shimmering in the window. The door was open, so I went inside to look around. Almost hidden on a rack of garments, I discovered an incredible straw-berry-red silk dress. On impulse I tried it on, and magically, it fit perfectly. As I twirled in front of the mirrors, I felt that I had never been more beautiful. Every detail of the dress burned itself into my memory and I happily fell asleep wearing that dress.

I couldn't forget about it. The dress haunted my thoughts and I constantly saw myself dancing in the Piazza San Marco wearing the strawberry-red dress. It wasn't until a week later, while driving across town, that I realized that I had to give "my" dress to Susan (the heroine in *Sono Claudio*). I stomped and raged about it for days, but that was another turning point in the writing of the story. From there I virtually flew to the ending—the happy, romantic ending.

Years ago I read a book that recommended—for those of us whose families never supported our dreams or offered the kind of encouragement we wanted—creating a fantasy family. They could be living or dead. So I did. It is a wonderful family, and I still call on some of them sometimes to help me. There was Uncle Vincent Van Gogh, who helped me with color. Uncle Fred Astaire danced with me and thought I was very graceful. Grandmother Eleanor Roosevelt encouraged me to be who I am. I chose Jane Fonda as my workout leader, but she was a little hard on me so I replaced her with Dolly Parton, who always called me "honey" as she coaxed me into exercising.

I got myself into a bit of trouble with my real family over my fictional family. I telephoned my daughter one day to say that I had a wonderful conversation with Uncle Vincent, and he had inspired me to create a new painting. I went on and on about how excited I was.

"Who's Uncle Vincent?" Laura inquired.

"Vincent Van Gogh," I replied.

"Mom, isn't he dead? How could you have a conversation with him?"

I tried to explain about my imaginary family, but I could tell Laura thought I'd stepped off the deep end.

A day or so later my son Tim called and asked in a very serious voice, "So, Mom, do you want to tell me about Uncle Vincent?'

I was amused by the whole incident, but I know for certain that I had them worried about my sanity for a while.

Months later, for Laura's birthday I gathered a big paint box with brushes, canvases, and other art supplies. I wrapped it all up in a plain brown package and tied it up with string. In what I hoped looked like Van Gogh's handwriting, I wrote: To Laura, Happy Birthday. Love, Uncle Vincent. Laura's longtime roommate took a look at it and asked, "Who's Uncle Vincent?"

I thought, if my imaginary family helped me so much, why not an imaginary literary group? I had had a falling out with my normal support group and had spent a couple of days on the pity-pot feeling like no one understood me. So I created a new group. I call them the Board of Directors. They consist of F. Scott Fitzgerald, who helps me weave romance and magic into my stories; Annie Lamott, who keeps me realistic about story and pacing; Charles Dickens, to help me with memorable characters; Rosamunde Pilcher, for her sense of place and ability to bring surroundings alive; and Maeve Binchy, for her ability to weave magic around normal, everyday people. I added Isabel Allende because she is so full of love and goodwill that she brings a healing energy over the whole group.

When I was much younger, my real family worried about my active imagination. My mother thought I spent too much time daydreaming. At one point in high school, I thought I was crazy because of all the characters I created and situations I made up. As an adult, I realize that those voices were telling me their stories so I would write them. Susan Paige and Julie Taylor are extensions of myself. I know that. But I also know that they are my best friends and will guide me in telling their stories.

But I've got to run, because right now the Board of Directors is pressuring me for the next chapter and Dolly is sweet-talking me into going out for a walk.

 Jacqueline Harmon Butler is the recipient of several press awards for her writing, including Italy's prestigious Golden Linchetto Prize for best foreign journalist. In a variety of international publications and anthologies, her travel writing has tempted readers' palates with mouthwatering meals. Her latest book is the sixth edition of *The Travel Writer's Handbook* (Surrey Books). For more information on her books, stories, and adventures, please visit www.jacquelineharmonbutler.com.

Don't Stop Believing
By Karin Tabke

"Don't Stop Believing," the signature song of the American rock band Journey, was written in 1981 and was used in the last diner scene of *The Sopranos*, which aired in 2007. The song has endured because its message is a good one. Here's why you never stop believing: because the minute you do, you lose something very precious. Hope. When you lose hope, you wither up and die. Hope is life. It's energy, it's adrenaline. It's the promise of success, of love, of grabbing the golden ring and hanging on for the wild ride.

What is Merriam-Webster's definition?

Hope (v.): to cherish a desire with anticipation; to desire with expectation of obtainment; to expect with confidence.

Believe (v.): to accept as true, genuine, or real; to have a firm conviction as to the goodness, efficacy, or ability of something.

Keep the hope alive. When hope is gone, the game is lost. Excitement and anticipation dry up. You are a shell. No juice inside. No heart, no soul. Nothing. Believing in yourself and hope go hand in hand. Without the belief that you will achieve your goal, there cannot be hope.

These emotions are not a craft. But hope and belief in ourselves can be learned and applied and—once mastered—can be the engine in your pursuit of publication, hitting the *New York Times* bestseller list, or whatever you choose to set as your goal. If you believe it will happen and hope it will happen, the engine is started. Now you put it into gear and start driving. A map helps, but sometimes even the best planned trips require taking an unexpected side road, turning around when a bridge is out, or perhaps deciding halfway into the trip you want to go somewhere else. Detours abound in life, but hope and belief keep us going.

It's okay to change your mind. It's okay to improvise when situations change. Finding your way means adapting to the block thrown in the road and overcoming it. Sometimes you can plow straight through it. Sometimes you have to build a bridge or tunnel beneath. Sometimes, you have to turn around and backtrack and go the really long way. Sometimes you find a really cool shortcut. But writing is indeed a journey, a trip, and a destination. As with any trip, you have to make it happen. You can't allow the winds of fate to sweep you away. You may end up somewhere you don't want to be.

Believe in yourself. And keep the hope, the faith, and the knowledge in your heart that you will arrive at your destination. Once there, look to the horizon for your next journey.

And don't stop believing.

Karin Tabke writes stories about empowered women and the hot cops who penetrate their lives. A full-time writer, Karin draws on a lifetime of stories and backdrops that few outside of the law enforcement community ever see, let alone hear. Controlled chaos reigns supreme through the pages she writes, where hot heroes serve, protect, and pleasure from page one to The End. Watch this summer for *Jaded*, the third book in her Hot Cops series, and *Master of Surrender*, the first book in her medieval The Blood Sword Legacy series.

Perseverance
By Lisa Hughey-Underwood

The literal definition of the word persevere is to continue in a course of action in spite of difficulty or lack of success. But this does not fully represent the relationship between perseverance and writing. Success means different things to different people. Lack of success encompasses more than just being unable to sell your book. As a writer, once you are published, your idea of success shifts and grows. After reaching the goal of having a manuscript published, perhaps success means attaining a spot on the *USA Today* Bestseller List, or making the *New York Times* Extended List, or hitting the *New York Times* top fifteen. Then success is moving up the list, and then staying on the list longer and longer. Perseverance isn't just something you need until you sell, and then you can let go. This quality must stay with you throughout your career. The path to perseverance is paved with three actions:

1.   Set intentions.
2.   Study craft.
3.   Celebrate your achievements.

An intention is a positive aim toward achievement and announces your determination to write, to submit, to study craft. At the very least, set intentions for your day and for your week. An intention can be as small as "I intend to write today" or as grand as "I intend to submit 10 queries this week." If you prefer to set concrete goals, that's fine. Just make sure your intentions and goals aren't totally unattainable. For instance, if you struggle to write 500 words a day, don't set a goal of 2,000 words a day. The purpose of a goal is to achieve something and feel motivated by your achievement. If you never achieve any of your goals, this will wear down your spirit. Also, you need to set goals that you alone can control. "I'm going to sell two books this year" is a goal you have very little control over. Try, "I am going to write and submit two books this year."

Find the process (intentions, goals, or both) that works for you. Take a few minutes at the beginning of your week and write down your intentions and goals. Post them someplace prominent, someplace where you will see them every day. On a daily basis, take a moment at the beginning of each writing session, before you place your hands on the keyboard, to review and set your intentions. This practice will keep your intentions and goals present in your mind.

Why study craft? Everyone from beginners to multi-published authors can learn from studying craft. There are always new insights into your writing psyche if you make the time to study the craft of writing. Everything we experience and learn informs our writing. Attend an informative writer's meeting. Discuss writing process with other writers. Analyze the book you just read for what worked and what didn't (this does not have to be a structured analysis—it can be as simple as defining the black moment, defining the characters and their relationship to each other, or taking a particular scene or passage and thinking about why it worked, or didn't, for you). Read books on process: *The Writer's Journey* by Christopher Vogler, *GMC: Goal, Motivation, and Conflict* by Debra Dixon, *Story* by Robert McKee. During each stage of your career, you will take away some new insight from instruction and study.

Beware of letting study time overtake your writing time, and don't use studying as an excuse never to make it to the page. Don't let lack of confidence in your writing influence your intention to write. But if that lack starts to overwhelm you, how do you keep writing day in and day out? How do you bring yourself to the keyboard time and time again? You have to find the validation and determination from within. In his book, *Writing from the Inside Out: Transforming Your Psychological Blocks to Release the Writer Within*, Dennis Palumbo reminds us emphatically: "You Are Enough." Let yourself be enough, take the study of craft, and settle at your keyboard.

Finally, celebrate each step that brings you closer to your goal. Celebrate finishing each manuscript, first in draft form and again when it is revised and revised and revised. Celebrate when you get a 9 in a contest, even if the other score was a 2. Celebrate when you get that request for an entire manuscript or even a partial. Celebrate when you get that first rejection letter that says, "I love your writing, but . . .". Celebrate when your editor loves it, even if her boss doesn't. Celebrate when the book hits the list, even if the ranking is less than you had hoped.

The celebration doesn't have to be a big deal. Treat yourself to a latte or a cinnamon twist. Buy a scented candle or plant a flower. Splurge on a glass of champagne with dinner or a trip to the office supply store. Just remember that along your writing journey, it is important to honor your accomplishments, honor your craft, honor yourself. All of these little celebrations mean one thing: You are writing. You are a writer.

And after you take that little bit of time to celebrate . . . go back to your keyboard or your research books or your revisions, and keep on writing. Because at the end of the day, week, month, year . . . perseverance is the act of sitting down at your pad of paper, your AlphaSmart™, or your keyboard to write, write, WRITE!

Lisa Hughey-Underwood continues to practice perseverance while she writes her seventh novel. When not focusing on her first love, romantic thrillers, she blogs about her second passion, saving the planet at www.365gogreen.com.

The Meaning of Persistence

By Jasmine Haynes, Jennifer Skully, and J.B. Skully
(Because it takes all three of us!)

I was a late bloomer. At least that's what I like to tell myself. Sounds better than saying I was a loser for eight years before I got published. Therein lies my message (for myself as well as everyone else). I was never a loser. Losers don't know the meaning of persistence. Losers stop trying, and when you stop trying, well, gee, it's all over, isn't it?

Before joining Romance Writers of America (RWA) in 1995, I had written several novels. I'd even sent them out, only to have them rejected. However, I wasn't persistent. I'd get one rejection and under the bed that book would go. I didn't have anyone else to read or critique for me, not even a family member, which probably isn't the best idea anyway. I just want my family to love everything I write even if they have to lie to me about it. I did take some writing classes during that time, but writing was still more of a hobby for me—until I got serious and joined RWA.

That's when I learned the meaning of persistence. That's when I realized I was never going to give up my writing. Even as I wallpapered my office with rejection letters, I knew writing was in my blood.

I'll admit that when I was in my twenties, I did quit writing. I'd tried without success to get some short stories published while in high school and college. I figured I'd never be a writer. But I was young, and what I hadn't learned yet was that you didn't need to be published to be a writer. The writer comes from within. A writer has a story to tell. And a writer must tell that story even if no one ever reads it. A writer is taken over by characters even if no one else knows those characters exist.

I learned that in 1998 when I started writing the Max Starr series. My character Max was a part of me. I was compelled to tell her story. She wouldn't let me go. I hadn't planned on a series, but once the first book was done, Max still wouldn't shut up. So I kept writing. I won contests with that first book, Dead to the Max, but I still couldn't find an agent or an editor. But Max, she made me keep writing until I had five books and a complete series. Okay, I even fell in love with my hero, Detective Witt Long, which is really scary. But that's another story.

That's when I realized I was a writer no matter what. That I would never stop writing. The stories would always be there, I would always keep writing them, and it didn't take a publisher to tell me who I was. But that didn't mean I didn't want a publisher or that I stopped striving to be published. Persistence is never giving up, but there's another element to it, too. It's doing what you have to do to get your work out there.

So again, I come back to RWA. I do not believe you can truly learn the craft of writing if you only write in a vacuum. Unless you're Jane Austen or Edgar Allan Poe reincarnated. Making up stories is a talent, a gift, a calling, but learning to put that story together cohesively and make it a good read is a craft. I took all the seminars and classes I could through RWA, attended conferences and workshops, and I found a great critique group. I began to learn the craft of writing. Learning your craft should never stop, not even after you get published.

RWA also taught me the business of writing. The first synopsis I sent to an agent (long before I joined RWA) was 66 pages long. I'd simply condensed my book. And I certainly hope that agent does not remember me! I entered contests for more feedback and also because the final round of many contests is judged by an agent or editor. I wanted to get my name and my writing voice out there. I volunteered for my RWA chapter. While doing good for the chapter, it also brought me in contact with agents and editors and other industry professionals. I always made pitch appointments whenever I went to a conference, honing my presentation skills as well as my writing skills.

And did I mention I never stopped writing? One book was finished, and off it went in a query. I always had five queries out at a time. While I was waiting to hear back, I started another book. Then another. And another as the years passed.

When the types of books I was writing didn't sell, I decided to try something new. I found my voice, over time, had become more comedic. I went from writing fairly dark romantic suspense to more of a romantic comedy. Of course, I still killed people, too. It was just in my nature. I also turned to erotic romance. Erotica wasn't my thing, but the erotic romance, now that had appeal. I'd never written shorter books, either, so writing a novella was a challenge.

And lo and behold, what did I sell first? Once of those novellas, to a new erotic romance imprint for an e-publisher, Liquidsilverbooks.com. It took eight years of persistence (since I'd joined RWA), but I had my first sale, *More Than a Night*, and Jasmine Haynes was born. Then, writing as J.B. Skully, I sold the Max Starr series to LiquidSilver. I wrote more novellas. I found an agent and sold my first romantic comedy to Harlequin later that year, and Jennifer Skully was born. *Sex and the Serial Killer* went on to win the 2006 Daphne du Maurier Award. Within six months of that sale, my agent sold some of my e-published novellas to Berkley. My second book for Berkley, *Somebody's Lover*, was a 2007 RITA Award finalist, and the next book, *Open Invitation*, won the Holt Medallion. And all those books I'd been working on for years and years started to see the light of day instead of the darkness of my hard drive. They weren't rotten books, but each one had a fatal flaw that kept it from selling. But now I had an agent and editor to concisely tell me how to fix those fatal flaws.

My brother once told me that when he looked up "persistence" in the dictionary, there was a picture of me beside it. I'm proud he noticed how persistent I was.

So, what is the meaning of persistence? Never stop writing, and never give up. Hone your craft—RWA is a great place to do it. Don't write in a vacuum. Find a critique partner or group. Learn the business of writing. Network. Volunteer. Try something new. It just might be the thing that works for you. And always, keep writing. When you finish one book, start another.

None of these activities should stop when you're published. There are always new subjects to learn, new ideas to try, new people to meet, and, best of all, new stories to write.

Jennifer Skully's romances bubble over with humor and self-discovery. As Jasmine Haynes, she writes spicy romance, and as J.B. Skully, she's created the Max Starr series. Visit Jennifer at www.skullybuzz.com. Look for Jasmine Haynes's trilogy: *The Fortune Hunter*, November 2007; *Show and Tell*, July 2008; and *Games People Play* in 2009.

PART II
CRAFT

"Stories have been told since the dawn of language. The focus of those tales has always been the people who inhabit them; events were re-counted only as a backdrop to the exploits of the heroes and heroines. From the earliest days, storytellers have known a simple truth: strong characters may carry a weak plot, but weak characters cannot be hidden by a strong plot."

-- *The Complete Writer's Guide to Heroes & Heroines: Sixteen Master Archetype*s by Tami D. Cowden, Caro LaFever, and Sue Viders

Breaking Rules
By Allison Brennan

If you enter a contest sponsored by any number of Romance Writers of America (RWA) chapters, you'll inevitably get a comment or two that says something like, "You can't do this" or "You must do that." The truth is, there is only one rule to writing.

Write.

Snide, I know. But you'll never sell if you don't write, and you'll never write if you tie yourself up in the "rules" that you had no part in creating.

Okay, just to get it out there: there are some things you do need to know. Basic grammar, sentence construction, paragraphs. All those things that you either know or don't know through years of school, reading, and writing. Yes, writing. The more you write, the better your writing.

I subscribe to Stephen King's opinion as stated in his must-read book, *On Writing*. To paraphrase, bad writers will never be competent writers, and competent writers will never be great writers, but competent writers can learn to be good writers. I'm going to assume that everyone reading this is at least a competent writer. You can put sentences together coherently and you understand the basic rules of grammar and that it's okay to break some of those rules for literary impact.

So you're a competent writer. Maybe you haven't sold yet, or maybe you've sold but you're stagnating. How can you rise to that next level—be it your first sale or your first breakout book?

First, my advice is to enrich your writer's tool chest. Stephen King goes into this in great detail, but what this means is to know all the tools at your disposal and use the right tools to most effectively get your story across. Read first, last, and always. Through reading a breadth of authors across many genres, you'll absorb the basic "rules" of storytelling. In addition, it doesn't hurt to brush up on what the experts say: King, Vogler, Maass, Dixon, others. You never know what little tidbit will give you that "aha!" moment that changes the way you write.

Second, know that it's always about the story. Without the story, you have no book. The story comes first. Story, story, story. Remember that and you can't go wrong.

And finally, you have to break the so-called "rules."

Your world, your rules.

Seems easy to remember, right? This is your book. You get to make the rules. Now, I wouldn't suggest taking out quotation marks because the reader should intuit where they go, but I will suggest that when you're building your story world, you get to decide when and where the hero and heroine first meet, be it the first chapter or the ninth. Just because one editor or one contest judge told you that you had to have your hero and heroine meet by the end of chapter one doesn't mean that they have to. If it's organic to the story, absolutely—in my book, *The Hunt*, Quinn and Miranda are on the same page before the end of chapter one. But in *Speak No Evil*, Nick and Carina couldn't be on the same page until chapter nine. The story wouldn't allow it. First and foremost: be true to the story.

Every author breaks different rules. Remember, your world, your rules. This doesn't mean you have to break the same rules I break. What it means is that rule breaking is an individual writer's choice—and has an impact on your unique authorial voice.

Be true to yourself and your voice.

Finding your voice can be hard. It might take a couple of manuscripts under the belt before you really "get it" or find that the rhythm is comfortable. This doesn't mean that it gets easier; what it means is that the story feels right. You've discovered your voice—the tone, the style, the rhythm all combined give you a unique voice. When you find it, you'll know.

And when you find it, do everything you can to protect it. Critique partners should be enhancing your voice—showing you the weakness in your manuscript that detracts from your natural voice—rather than trying to squash your voice. A good critique group is worth its weight in royalties . . . a bad critique group can kill your voice. So be discerning.

Be fair to other authors.

I have heard comments ad nauseum from readers and writers who criticize published authors, not for the quality of the story, but for breaking rules. You will never please all the people all the time. You have to accept that and learn to live with it. You must please yourself. You must please your agent and editor. You must please your core readership. But not all romance readers are your core readership. It's hard sometimes to take criticism, but a thick skin is necessary in this business.

I've heard from people that "well, she's Nora Roberts, of course she can head hop." No, she can't. She can head hop because she does it well. I've read a lot of Nora Roberts/J.D. Robb books and I don't get pulled out of the story when she head hops. She's that good. If head hopping comes naturally to you, use it—if you're that good.

That's the "rule" of rule breaking. Any rule can be broken if it's done well. So be fair to other authors. Nora Roberts doesn't "get away" with head hopping because she's Nora. She uses it effectively.

Listen to your editor.

If you have the benefit of an editor, listen to her. In my limited time in this business, I've learned one crucial fact about editors. They know when something is wrong. They may not know how to fix it, but a good editor knows a problem when they see it. Listen to that. You might not agree with their solution—they may not even offer one—but definitely address these areas of the manuscript.

To relate this to critique partners (CP), they don't know everything. But if your three CPs all have a problem with a scene, trust me—there's a problem. It might not be with that scene. It might be with the chapter before it and that scene highlighted that your characters are "out of character" or that you didn't establish character well enough at the beginning for them to buy into the scene. You need to listen and then . . .

Trust your instincts.

You must trust your instincts in all parts of the process, from the creation to the editing to the problems. You may be too close to the story to see a problem, but you also know where you want the story to go. Therefore, listen and consider the advice of your editor and critique partners, but in the end you must do what is best for the story.

Discerning criticism.

Writing isn't easy. Getting published isn't easy. This is a tough business made tougher by the fact that writing is a creative pursuit—our ideas, the things and people we care about, go into the crafting of our stories. Criticism is hard to take, but all competent writers must at some point send their baby out there and take the lumps.

Here's my quick list of questions to ask when you get back a critique from a contest, a critique partner, or even an editor or agent.

- Does it make your writing stronger?
- Does it make your story stronger?
- Is it a "rule" or suggestion?
- Does it enhance or diminish your voice?
- Does it make sense to you?

If the advice makes sense to you, if you hit yourself on the head and think, "Damn, why didn't I think of that?" then it's probably good advice. But if you're making changes because you think that the critiquer is somehow better than you, knows your story better than you, or because they marked "published author" on their judging form and therefore they must know better than you, then you're doing the wrong thing. You have to believe in every change you commit to your book. Remember that: your book. This is your book, your story, your characters.

I'm not saying never take advice. The critique group I had before I sold taught me so much about myself and my writing. I became a much stronger writer because of them. But I didn't do everything they suggested. Instead, I weighed the advice and decided if it fit with my vision for the story. And sometimes, neutral eyes can give you a new perspective on your work.

But the truth is, one editor can reject a book for all the reasons that another editor falls in love with it. To edit to please only one person (unless, of course, that person is your editor and they've already paid you money to write and revise the book) is foolhardy. Don't do it. Learn to separate the wheat from the chaff — the good advice from the bad. I can't tell you how to do it. But if you follow my five-point outline above, it gives you a good start.

It's all subjective.

My debut novel was rejected. On the same day I signed with one agent, another agent rejected it with a list of perceived problems — and some of them I did end up fixing in editor revisions. But some of the suggestions would have completely changed the tone of the story. This isn't to say you shouldn't make agent changes — if you agree with them. If they make the story stronger. But remember that not everyone has the same taste. Not everyone has the same vision for a book. That doesn't make them right or wrong. It doesn't make you right or wrong.

Be true to your voice and trust your instincts, learn when to take advice and when to leave it, but most important . . . Forget rules and just write!

Allison Brennan is the *New York Times* bestselling author of eight romantic thrillers. Her current book is *Tempting Evil; Sudden Death* is available in October. She lives in Northern California with her husband and five kids.

Finding Your High Concept
By Jenny Andersen

Having a high concept makes a story easier to sell. But exactly what is high concept? High concept isn't a hook, a blurb, or a pitch. It isn't your story in 25 words or less. High concept is the central, core idea of a story that is universally and emotionally exciting to a wide audience.

Ideas and themes that are common to many readers lend themselves to high-concept stories. For instance, dinosaurs, the struggle to lose weight, vampires, magic, stalking, sex, and snakes are subjects of universal interest that can be turned into high-concept ideas by incorporating a fresh twist.

For example, say there's a big earthquake in California. As it is, no big deal. California has earthquakes all the time. The twist is missing, as is the human element.

Try again: A big earthquake in San Francisco rumbles under San Quentin, freeing the prisoners. Scores of dangerous criminals are turned loose on a society in turmoil.

Much better.

Something more is required, however. The emotionally exciting human element is still missing. To make this idea tempting, the reader has to care about the characters. If your protagonist is a reporter and he hears about the earthquake and subsequent escape while he's in Chicago on another story . . . well, ho-hum. If, instead, your protagonist is a young woman who is stranded (for a good reason, please) on the road next to the prison at the wrong moment, you'll hook a lot of readers.

The first page of your book, the inciting incident, has to plunge a likable character into action in a way that resonates with those readers. Does that young woman stand beside her disabled car while several escaped prisoners take her hostage or does she . . . ? What could she do? Time to brainstorm!

Start with a universally appealing and emotionally exciting idea, give it an unusual twist, and you'll have a high-concept story.

Take the High Concept Quiz!
Name these high-concept movies.

1. A bomb on board a bus will explode if the bus goes less than 50 miles per hour.
2. A cop and a criminal switch faces.
3. An ordinary man trades places with God.
4. A man must live the same day over and over.

5. Poisonous snakes get loose on an airplane.
6. A troubled teen comes to terms with life.
7. A woman's past comes back to haunt her.
8. A boy discovers he is a wizard.

Answers:

1. Speed
2. Face/Off
3. Bruce Almighty
4. Groundhog Day
5. Snakes on a Plane
6. and 7. No high concept—there are dozens of movies that fit these descriptions.
8. Harry Potter and the Sorcerer's Stone

Thanks to Allison Brennan for the prison idea. Jenny Andersen had her first (and only) play produced when she was eight, by a neighbor whose kids were the actors. Years later, she's published scientific research papers and short fiction, but is still pursuing the novel sale. In her spare time, she sells antique jewelry, plays the harp, and enjoys life with the world's best DH.

Plotting, Plotting, Plotting
By Alexandra Singer

I started my first novel as a pantser—I didn't think much about where I ultimately needed to end up, and just wrote and wrote. And wrote. It never ended! I was unemployed, so I had tons of time on my hands, but my method clearly wasn't working—I was aimless and so was the story. And the threads that absolutely needed to be interwoven throughout a novel so they can be brought together and tied up at the end simply weren't there. Of course, pantsers will argue, you can layer that stuff in during the editing process, but that's way more time-consuming and convoluted than having a simple outline in the first place.

So, I'd like to come out as a former pantser and now big-time advocate of the plot outline—the more detailed the better! It doesn't matter to me whether you prefer charting character arcs on the wall, or writing out a 10-page outline in synopsis form, or doing a scene-by-scene recap with different colors for different plot points (one for emotion, one for conflict, one for sensuality, and so on). Whatever works for you. Some type of outline will help you clarify where you're going with your plot and characters.

And of course, if you discover the direction you've outlined is just plain wrong, feel free to change it. We shouldn't be wedded to plots and characters that don't feel right just because we've lived together for a little while. What sounds fabulous in a synopsis may not resonate or fulfill when fully fleshed out into a story.

But I've learned from experience that you shouldn't simply change the story you're writing—make the plot changes to the outline, as well, when the muse quiets down and you're no longer engrossed in the writing part of the process. Then, as you continue with the nitty-gritty of writing your novel, you'll always have a tour guide for the road ahead.

Alexandra Singer toils as a direct marketing consultant by day, and by night spins turn-of-the-century Belle Epoque romantic fantasies set in Paris, Marrakesh, and Tunis. She lives in Berkeley, CA with her husband, Ali; new baby, Mina; and calico cat, Whispers. Visit www.alexandrasinger.com for excerpts from her trilogy and other goodies.

Building Your Book with Theme, Motif, and Metaphor
by Shelley Adina

Have you ever received a letter from an editor that said, "I liked your characters and your ideas, but the story just didn't seem to hang together"? You spent days rereading it, and even took it to your critique group, but you couldn't figure out what the editor meant or how you could fix your manuscript. Well, maybe she was looking for something deeper than merely what happened in the plot. Maybe she was looking for a story with a theme, supported by the use of images, symbols, and metaphor. Let's look at how these can help to form the structure of your novel, make it cohesive, and give it meaning.

So what is theme? It's the central idea that you're trying to prove through the story events and the actions of your characters. In one of the very helpful articles on her website, Alicia Rasley says, "When you examine the same issue in different books, you don't use precisely the same theme. Think of the issue as the general question, and the theme as the answer particular to this book—to this plot and this set of characters." The All About Us series of young adult novels I write for the Christian market all deal with a similar issue that's encapsulated in my tagline: God, girlfriends, and a designer handbag. What more do you need to survive high school? But the theme of each book is different. In one, the theme is "God shows us our real friends through the power of discernment." In another, "The power of honesty can set us free."

Once you know your central idea or theme, you can tie all the pretty stuff—the images, motifs, and so on—into it. What this does is create cohesion in your descriptions and settings that can give your book a sense of its own completeness. You won't find yourself wandering off into thickets of narrative that don't contribute directly to your story. Instead, it will look as though it grew organically. "Write tight" doesn't just mean hunting down adjectives and adverbs with a red pen and making them bleed. It means choosing only words and phrases that contribute somehow to your theme—that form the metaphors and images that support it.

So what's a metaphor? Jennifer Crusie defines it perfectly in "The Five Things I've Learned About Writing Romance from TV," one of the articles on her website.

> In the *Gilmore Girls* TV show, Lorelei's daughter, Rory, got a car from her boyfriend, Dean. He restored it himself, working on it for two TV seasons, and as a metaphor for someone who wants to help her leave home safely, it's a beaut. In the same episode,

her loving grandfather throws a fit because Dean is giving the
car to her and goes with him to have it safety checked over and
over again, selling the metaphor from a different perspective:
He has to be convinced it's safe for Rory to leave. Spelled out
like that, it's important, but it's also a big yawn. Demonstrated
in two characters fighting over a car while a bored mechanic
says, "Can I please go home now?" it's funny and touching and
a beautiful demonstration of love.

In other words, metaphor in novels can be illustrated in subtext, or what's really happening behind "what's happening." In Crusie's view, a person doesn't write about a coffee table. She writes about what's under it. Here's an example. Say your teenage character is arguing with her mother about what color to paint her room. On paper, the argument may be about crimson versus cream. But in the reader's mind, you're building an argument about control—of personal space, of the speed at which the girl is growing up, of the ability to make one's own decisions. You can show these things through the vehicle of the argument without actually saying a word about control or growing up. And you can even use the colors—crimson, cream—as a tiny symbol that can speak volumes about the girl's blossoming personality and sexuality versus the mother's—and the latter's fear of them.

In the All About Us series, I use theme and metaphor as an underlay to all the teenage drama going on at the surface. The plot of the first book, *It's All About Us* (FaithWords, May 2008), is simple: A Christian teenager at a posh private school considers becoming a "technical virgin" so she can keep her boyfriend. She's also struggling with an internal question: Should she keep her faith under wraps in order to be friends with the cool kids? But the central theme is deeper than these two plotlines; it's derived from Philippians 1:9-10, which is about the power of discernment. In each book, the different protagonists learn a scriptural power that they can own and use as they reappear throughout the series.

This gives me a number of interesting metaphors and motifs that I can own and use, too. For instance, in *It's All About Us*, my heroine wears contact lenses, and she wouldn't be caught dead in public in her glasses. She's short-sighted both in a physical sense and in a metaphorical sense, because she's dazzled by the prospect of popularity and the good looks of the most popular boy in school as he becomes interested in her. She sees externals (like fashion, makeup and hair, and money) first, at the expense of other characters' internal value. Lastly, I can apply my theme to the setting, which is the Pacific Heights neighborhood of San Francisco. The reader finds fog rolling in during the heroine's periods of obscured vision.

In the second book, *The Fruit of My Lipstick* (FaithWords, August 2008), the title, the cover art, and the theme are derived from Hebrews 13:15–16, which talks about the "fruit of our lips giving praise to His name." The heroine is a self-described "loud Asian chick" who is able to speak out about her faith and whose reputation for academic brilliance speaks loud and clear. But she falls for a guy who takes away her voice by undermining her self-confidence and her very self-image, molding her to his idea of the meek, quiet Asian girl. The plot events and character behaviors center around this dismantling process—which she isn't even aware of because of her inexperience and insecurity. On the underlying level, the book is about the protagonist learning the power of honesty, not just loudness, both with herself and with her friends.

See how theme, metaphor, and symbolism all tie together? Sit down with your manuscript and give its central theme some thought—and then work with your descriptions, metaphors, and subtext to give your story its own unique flavor and sense of wholeness. Your readers—including that editor—will thank you!

 RITA Award–winning author Shelley Adina is a world traveler and pop culture geek with an incurable addiction to designer handbags. She holds an M.A. in Writing Popular Fiction from Seton Hill University, and is delighted to be the launch author for the FaithWords teen books. Between books, Shelley loves traveling, listening to and making music, and creating period costumes.

Getting the Author Off the Page
By Alice Gaines

There I was, about halfway through writing my first book. My heroine, Rory McDermott, was sitting in the coach's booth at a minor league professional football game. She'd just suggested a play to the head coach. And, I wrote, Down on the field, Sidewinder put on his helmet and ran into the game.

I stopped writing and stared at the sentence. I knew enough about writing to realize I was supposed to be showing the story through my main character's eyes. I wasn't supposed to be reporting dry facts or, worse, telling Sidewinder's story. Still, that sentence worked. In fact, it worked far better than the alternative, Rory watched Sidewinder put on his helmet and run into the game. Why?

Over the years, the revelation I had that day came to fit in a category that I call "getting the author off the page." Others call it deep point of view and various other things. I love deep point of view and practice it as best I can. Nothing else does more to make a reader love the characters or to allow her to share in the characters' emotions.

I've developed some guidelines for myself, and I've shared them with contestants whose entries I've judged in contests. They might help you, too. Please note that these are not rules. Rules accomplish little besides making writers uncomfortable, and we do that to ourselves without any help. In fact, I'll give examples of when you should violate my guidelines. If you spent your hard-earned money for this book, you might want to let my ideas float around in your head and see if they make sense to you.

There are three broad categories of verbs that remove us one or more steps from experiencing the character's life directly. They are sensing, thinking, and emoting verbs.

- Sensing: To sense, feel, hear, smell, touch, taste, and others.
- Thinking: To think, realize, imagine, wonder, ponder, muse, be puzzled or confused, and others.
- Emoting: To feel, hate, fear, mourn, or to be angry, full of rage, sad, frightened, hopeless, and others.

For example: Your heroine is running for her life from the bad guy. She has ducked into an alley and hidden in a doorway, hoping he'll go by without finding her. You could write, She could feel her heart pounding in her chest and hear his footsteps approaching. Fear washed over her. The first two are sensing verbs, and the third is a variant of an emoting verb. This passage has the author telling (oops, that word) what's going on inside the heroine rather than letting the reader experience it directly.

As a reader, I'd much prefer, Her heart thundered in her chest as his footsteps approached. Damn, this had to work. If he found her, he'd cut her to ribbons. A few more details of what his footsteps sound like and the gruesome way he'd kill her would probably make the passage more compelling, but I hope you catch my drift. If done correctly, this method eliminates the reporter (the writer) and puts the reader directly in touch with the heroine.

Here's another one we see in romance a lot: What, she wondered, was he thinking? We shouldn't have to be told who's doing the wondering. We should know whose head we're in. What was he thinking? is far more direct. Or work in some clues to how she feels about his behavior. What in blue blazes was the stupid man thinking? Notice that you've shown that the heroine is angry because she's cursed with blue blazes. And, you know she thinks he's stupid or at least that he's acting stupid now.

When you get right down to it, people often deny their emotions, especially negative ones like anger and jealousy. This gives us a wonderful tool as writers. The character can be obviously upset about something and refuse to admit it. You've all seen this in real life. Someone scowling, wagging her foot and declaring, "I'm not mad. If he wants to make an idiot of himself in front of the entire company, that's his business." And, we all know how much fun it is when the heroine refuses to face the fact that she finds the hero attractive. We know better, and honestly, she does, too. She just won't admit it.

Here's one from my own writing. Isabel Clinton cursed her luck. That's not horrid, but it's still me telling the reader that Isabel feels she has bad luck. Cursed luck gets the point across better. Of course, you want to follow with the details of her accursed luck, as in, Cursed luck. Isabel Clinton had sat for X days on a stiff train car seat only to arrive in Oakland, California, in the middle of a heat wave. One hundred degrees, the conductor had said. It might as well be Hades.

I must confess that I almost broke one of my nonrules here. I almost wrote, It felt like Hades. People do occasionally think about their own perceptions, thoughts, and emotions. If you visit my house in the winter, you might be tempted to say, "It feels like a refrigerator in here." So, this feels like a good place to discuss noncompliance with my nonrules.

At the beginning of a new scene, you need to clue the reader in to whose point of view they're in. If I were to start a scene with Down on the field, Sidewinder put on his helmet and ran into the game, you'd have to assume this is Sidewinder's story. Rory watched as or Rory's stomach clenched as would let the reader know we're with Rory.

In the case of What, she wondered, was he thinking? the author might want the she wondered to make the rhythm of the sentence work. Rhythm is very important in writing, especially in comedy. I think we've all seen this one overdone, though, and it gets quite cloying.

You might want to use sensing, thinking, and emoting verbs for emphasis.

Suppose the husband has just denied being at the No Tell Motel the night before. It would be perfectly logical for the wife to think, She knew he'd been there. She'd seen his car in the parking lot.

Finally, sometimes there's just no other way to say something without tying yourself—and your reader—into knots.

So, how can you tell when to avoid sensing, thinking, and emoting verbs? My suggestion is that when you find yourself writing, She saw a plume of smoke on the horizon, or She knew he wasn't telling the truth, or The sound terrified her, you stop and take a look at the passage and see if there isn't a more convincing way to create the image you're reaching for. It may be that A plume of smoke appeared on the horizon, or Lying came naturally to him, it seemed, or Damn! What was that sound? Had someone broken in the back door? will do a better job for you.

Award-winning author Alice Gaines writes erotic romance for Changeling Press, Ellora's Cave, and Red Sage, and contemporary romance and straight fantasy for Cerridwen Press. Her first erotic romance for Harlequin Spice Briefs (in electronic format) will appear in early 2008. A Victorian, the story is tentatively titled *The Well-Tutored Lover*. Alice holds a Ph.D. in personality psychology from the University of California at Berkeley. She lives and gardens in Oakland, California, and shares her life with two stray cats, Twitter and Cat-hole, and two delightful pet corn snakes, Casper and Sheikh Yerbouti. Alice loves to hear from readers at algaines@pacbell.net. Her website is http://home.pacbell.net/halice. For her online newsletter, send an e-mail to: AliceGainesChambers-subscribe@yahoogroups.com.

Bringing Characters to Life
by Kate Douglas

The plot is terrific, the setting ideal, but the characters have all the life of cardboard cutouts. You've taken them through their paces, but there's no sense of real flesh and blood. Physically perfect, yet lacking heart and emotion, they're not real. You don't feel a connection to your heroine and your hero doesn't make your heart race . . . and if you don't care what happens to your creations, how do you expect a reader to care?

So, how do you fix something you can't really nail down? I have a couple of tricks I've used over the years that still help me when I sense that the heart of the character I'm writing isn't beating.

Change the point of view.

You've written a scene from Mack's point of view and there's something lacking. Take that same scene and put it in Millie's POV. Find out what she sees, hears, tastes, or feels. Sometimes the simple act of changing POV will give you an entirely new feel for your character, and when you go back to the POV your story demands, you'll have new insight into your characters' motivations and reason for action—or inaction.

Become your character.

It's simpler than it sounds. Take a moment and close your eyes. Think of the situation your hero is in. Mack's facing the biggest threat in his life, Millie's angry with him, the killer is creeping up behind the fence where he's hiding, and this is his last chance to prove his worth, save the girl, and take out the bad guy. Now become Mack. What do you hear? How do you feel when a branch snaps behind you, the owl overhead suddenly takes flight? What does your skin feel? Cold, mist, hot and humid air, a chill wind? How does the temperature make your body react? Is there sweat running under your arms and down your sides? Are you afraid? Cocky and self-assured? Sexually aroused?

Let your thoughts wander to encompass anything you might experience while crouched behind a wooden fence with nothing more than a piece of wood in your hand for protection . . . or maybe you're holding a gun and the sweat on your palm makes you afraid the weapon will slip in your grasp. The options are endless. Consider your scene and then dig into your character's reactions to everything you can imagine. You don't need to use all of the points you come up with, but the mere fact you've considered them and felt them yourself helps round out the character crouched in the dark on the hard-packed ground, waiting for the killer.

Interview your characters.

I read this one years ago in the Romance Writers Report (the RWA member magazine) and have used it ever since. Sit down with a list of questions and interview all your main characters. How old are they, what birth order, how many brothers and sisters? Where did they grow up, what are their hobbies, who was their first love? Any questions you can think of will help you get to know your character better, and when you know them well enough, it's almost impossible to write "cardboard." You may never use the information you discover by answering the questions, but just knowing it helps you to write about a multidimensional character instead of someone without any depth.

For instance, have you ever thought of your character's politics? In most cases, that's something you'd never mention in a story, but if you as the author know your character's political leanings, that tells you things about them you might not otherwise have known. And you might be surprised when you pose those interview questions to discover things about your character you'd not known before.

As an example, I have an African-American hero in my book, *Wolf Tales IV*. Tinker McClintock has appeared in other stories in the series as a secondary character, but some of his personality traits were inconsistent, I thought, for a powerful Chanku shapeshifter. When I interviewed him, I suddenly discovered he'd grown up in a foster care system, raised by a white family until he was fifteen. He lived in a very nice middle-class neighborhood where he went to good schools and had lots of friends, but he'd never faced racism, never learned the realities of the real world as do many young black men. Then his foster parents were killed and Tinker was thrust into the system again, but without the background he needed to survive. Fifteen years old and an outcast in his own racial society, he learned to protect himself and his feelings, but he always felt as if he existed just outside whatever community embraced him. Even as Chanku, loved by his packmates, he knows he is different. These traits existed in the character before the interview, but they finally made sense to me afterward. Tinker went from being a secondary character to one with the depth and heart of a hero.

Write in the first person.

This is another method of becoming your character. You've got a scene that lacks life and emotion. Rewrite the scene in the first person, and while you're writing, you can't help but become that character. It's amazing how the mere act of starting a sentence with I can change the way you feel about the words you choose. It can give you a personal link to your character, points you might have missed otherwise. The process will often breathe new life into someone you've written from the distance of third person.

These are simple tricks and are not all that technical, but they're little steps that have helped me with every story I write. It comes down to something I learned when I was a newspaper reporter. If you ask the right questions, your subject will write your story for you. The same thing works in fiction. If you know your characters well enough, they'll tell their own tales. Good fiction isn't the author's story to tell. It belongs to the characters she creates. When those characters take on a life of their own, you know you've got a winner.

Kate Douglas has been writing for publication, in one form or another, her entire adult life. She is the lead author for Kensington Publishing's Aphrodisia imprint with her best-selling erotic paranormal series, Wolf Tales. Her upcoming book is *Wolf Tales VI*.

Five Reasons We Love that Bad Boy (with the Heart of Gold)

By Josie Brown

All I really need to know about writing romance novels I learned by reading *Gone With The Wind* (something I did thirteen times before reaching my sixteenth birthday). Margaret Mitchell's heroine, that now-classic rebel belle Scarlett O'Hara, may carry a 1,048-page-long torch for the morally upstanding Ashley Wilkes, but her readers know that Rhett Butler—the one person Scarlett scorns more than anyone else—is the only man who has the wit, guts, and passion to match this über-heroine.

Writing about bad boys is a lot of fun. We authors live vicariously through the mean men we create: guys who do the kind of things that awe and titillate us—and perhaps even repulse us, should we run into these guys in our own lives. The most fun I had with my newest Avon release, the glam-packed *Impossibly Tongue-Tied*, was writing about Sam Godwin, the Hollywood player and talent agent who can—and does—have any woman he wants. But Sam falls head-over-heels in love at first sight with my heroine, Nina Harte, a sweetly naive grocery store clerk, who, by the way, also happens to be happily married—

To (horrors!) a struggling actor, no less.

Then things get really complicated when Sam signs Nina's husband, Nathan, as a client. According to "O," the sultry phone-sex operator to whom Sam can't help but confess all, it's because his lady-love is so unattainable that has Sam so hot and bothered. Is she right? Sam refuses to believe that this is the case. He insists that Nina's innocence is the attraction; that, unlike most women he's met in Hollywood, Nina is totally without an agenda . . . which is why he is in constant turmoil over his instincts to take what he wants—Nina—particularly when he sees Nathan falling for the co-star in his first major film, Katerina McPherson.

Of course, Sam feels differently—to put it mildly, used, abused, and thoroughly played—when he discovers that "O" and Nina are one and the same.

Most authors will tell you that writing about bad boys is a blast. We've seen (and maybe even dated) this guy in real life, and we're always intrigued by his dark side, his backstory, and his motives. And of course, we know just how to fix him, to heal his pain—which is why putting him on the page is such a joy.

In my own research on such characters, I've picked up on five major traits that every Rhett—or Sam—seems to embody:

Trait 1. He is a handsome, callous heartbreaker. But isn't that part of his charm?

Trait 2. He may be ruthless, but he also has a heart of gold.

Trait 3. He acts out of anger, and then regrets the fact that he let his emotions—for her—get the better of him.

Trait 4. He allows us to live vicariously through him. He may ruin or kill, but somehow he earns our grudging respect. (And he certainly gets us all hot and bothered!)

Trait 5. He can be redeemed—by the right woman, of course!

So, who is your favorite bad boy, and why?

Josie Brown's glam lit novels are *Impossibly Tongue-Tied* (Avon) and *True Hollywood Lies* (Avon). You can read her books at her blog: www.josiebrown.com and email her at JosieBrownAuthor@yahoo.com.

Best Character Development Tools

By Clare Langley-Hawthorne

Characters and well-drawn character development lie at the heart of any good story. Many new writers, however, can feel intimidated by the issue of character development—where do you start? How do you create an arc for your characters so they can grow and change as the story progresses? What tools can a writer use to focus on characters and their development?

I have found that the best approach to these questions comes from adopting a two-stage process. First, I create a profile for each character, including name, physical profile, and background. Then I develop a broad character "map" for how I want my main characters to change and grow as the story unfolds.

Character Profile

As a visual person, I usually "see" my characters before I have any kind of plot established, so the first thing I do is write down a detailed physical description of the character and brainstorm a series of adjectives I would use to describe each one. Then, before I do anything else, I name the character. A name can convey a great deal about a character and for me this is an important step in solidifying him or her in my head.

I then build upon this by creating a short biography detailing information such as when and where they were born, their parents and background, education, and key past experiences. I include everything I can think of that will help establish the character for me and the reader. This profile provides a constant reference as I start to write the story. Characters, like us, are really the sum of their (albeit fictional) experiences, and so their background will color what they say, how they act (and react) to events, and how they behave and interact with other characters.

Character Map

The Character Map is a critical step in planning and outlining my stories. (And yes, I admit it, I'm someone who outlines!) I list my main characters on a large piece of paper and graph how I want the characters to develop as the plot progresses. I need to establish where they are in the beginning and where they will end up at the end of the book, both in terms of the plot as well as their characters.

In my first book, *Consequences of Sin*, for example, I knew I wanted my heroine, Ursula Marlow, to be transformed by the events in the book from a young, sheltered, and idealistic woman to a more independent woman who is self-reliant, determined, and yet also more vulnerable as a result of her experiences. Likewise,

71

I needed the hero, Lord Oliver Wrotham, to change as the plot unfolded so that by the end of the book, both he and Ursula can accept each other in love as equals (which they could never have done at the beginning). To achieve this I had to know, at least in a broad sense, how I wanted my characters to evolve through the key events in the book. While I didn't necessarily have all the details, I did have the arc along which my characters would travel.

These first two steps are by no means the end of the process. As I start writing, the story takes over and scenes and events alter my characters in ways I could never have predicted. So although I like to start out with a broad map, I find myself changing course a number of times and my characters quite regularly surprise me!

While writing, further issues relating to character development arise. These usually revolve around establishing a balance between showing and telling information about the character. I find that this balance is best achieved by constantly asking myself:

- What do I need to tell the reader directly, or what can be shown through the character's actions, mannerisms, and speech instead?
- How can I let the reader know key information about a character's background without breaking the narrative with a long (and possibly boring) exposition? Can I introduce it through dialogue?
- Can I intersperse background information gradually so the reader learns more and more as the plot unfolds? Will this help build a richer picture of the character over time?
- How can I demonstrate changes in a character's inner life (their thoughts and feelings) over the course of the story in a compelling way?

I much prefer to use dialogue and action to illustrate character development. I like to visualize each scene and think about how I can show more about my characters as the book unfolds. As I write the story, I constantly refer back to and refine my plot and character maps. In the editing phase, I ask myself how I can best use each scene, event, and interaction to draw out the nuances of each character so they can come alive for the reader. It's a constant process, but I find the first two steps—developing the Character Profile and Character Map—are invaluable tools to establishing strong, believable characters who will grow along with my story.

Clare Langley-Hawthorne was raised in England and Australia. She was an attorney in Melbourne before moving to the United States, where she began her career as a writer. Her first novel, *Consequences of Sin*, was published in February 2007, and is the first in an Edwardian mystery series featuring the Oxford graduate, heiress, and militant suffragette, Ursula Marlow. The second book in the series, *The Serpent and the Scorpion*, is an August 2008 release.

Feeding Your Muse: What Characters Eat

By Jacqueline Harmon Butler

You've heard the old adage, "The way to a man's heart is through his stomach." But have you heard the parallel writer's adage, "The way to a reader's heart is through their gastronomic senses"?

Step 1: Bring the reader to the table with your character. Many beginning writers make the mistake of merely listing the foods. Yes, a dinner of steak, baked potatoes, green beans, bread and butter, and iced tea sounds delicious. But that's a menu, not a meal. By seasoning this dinner with a few tempting details, you enable your reader to taste this scrumptious repast along with your character. Let's spice up your steak with a black peppercorn marinade and grill it to a juicy medium rare; add sour cream and freshly chopped chives to the baked potato; top your green beans with sautéed wild mushrooms, and let sweet butter drip over the edges of your fragrant sourdough French bread. Drop a sprig of fresh mint into your iced tea, and now both your character and your reader are enjoying this mouthwatering feast.

Step 2: Be adventurous. There is more to life than the standard American meat-and-potatoes fare. Take your reader on a vicarious culinary world tour. Consider incorporating some of these regional cuisines: African, Asian, Caribbean, French, Greek, Hungarian, Indian, Italian, Mexican, Middle Eastern, or Spanish. Each conjures images of delectable delights associated with distinctive smells and flavors.

Step 3: Know your ingredients. Mention a few of the prominent spices and herbs in your prose. For instance, much African cuisine comes from the area of Morocco and is associated with cumin or coriander; Italian is associated with basil, oregano, and garlic. French cooking is associated with heavy sauces seasoned with tarragon or chervil, à la the classic Béarnaise sauce. Greek food invokes flavors of olives and lemons. When you think Mexican, you think cilantro and chili peppers. When you serve your readers exotic fare, be sure to mention of some of the savory ingredients used in preparation. Don't give the entire recipe, just hint at some of its more flavorful herbs and spices.

Step 4: Remember that man (or woman) does not live by dinner alone. It's a refreshing change to serve an occasional breakfast, lunch, or brunch. Or take your character to a cocktail party and tease your reader with the textures and tastes associated with hors d'oeuvres and buffets.

Step 5: Dessert presents an incredible assortment of ideas. Where to serve the dessert is limitless and the images conjured up by a situation can be extremely stimulating. Most people find licking a spoon of chocolate mousse or eating fresh, fragrant strawberries very sexy.

Step 6: Remember to round out your imaginary meal with beverages. An ice-cold, fizzy soda; tangy juice; perfectly aged Chianti; a chilled glass of champagne; or maybe a cozy, hot Irish coffee complement the scene.

At this point, you may be throwing your hands in the air and saying, "But I can't even boil water without burning it!" Don't despair. You don't have to be a gourmet chef to create illusory cuisine. A little research will have you cooking up literary feasts that will have even the most discerning palates begging for seconds. As long as you can read a cookbook or surf the web, you can write tantalizing passages. Often, tried-and-true menus are already assembled, so you don't have to worry about confusing or overwhelming the palate.

Better yet, spend an afternoon on the sofa with your television tuned to one of those 24-hour cooking stations. Incorporating little details regarding the preparation process can make your story not only seem real, but educational, too. But when it comes to research, I can't say enough about the advantages of field trips. What a great excuse to visit a five-star restaurant and sample some glamorous dishes. Or visit a late-night café or take-out delicatessen. This kind of research is considered tax-deductible, too.

So, what's on the menu for your hero tonight? Maybe a wild salmon steak with a sprinkling of capers and sliced lemon, presented on a bed of al dente fettuccine seasoned with garlic and olive oil? A salad of fresh field greens with a tangy Italian dressing and a bottle of Napa Valley Zinfandel? Accent the meal with some crusty bread spread with country-style butter and you have a recipe for more than dinner. Add a few other sensory details, like candlelight, fine china, soft music, and let's just say, they might not get around to dessert.

Jacqueline Harmon Butler is the recipient of several press awards for her writing, including Italy's prestigious Golden Linchetto Prize for best foreign journalist. In a variety of international publications and anthologies, her travel writing has tempted readers' palates with mouthwatering meals. Her latest book is the sixth edition of *The Travel Writer's Handbook* (Surrey Books). For more information, visit www.jacquelineharmonbutler.com.

Adding Vividness to your Writing

By Madelyn Bello

Common questions writers hear are "Where do you get your story ideas?" and "How do you make your stories so real?" My answer to both questions is "everywhere."

I once took a self-defense class. The teacher taught the three A's of self-defense: awareness of our surroundings, alertness to changes in our surroundings, and actions we could take to ensure our survival. The three A's can also be applied to recognizing story ideas and actions, expressions, or mannerisms that can enrich our writing.

Be Aware.

Be aware of your surroundings and mine the area for ideas. Inspiration can spark from observing a person's mannerisms to hearing an unusual speech pattern and wanting to capture that for your character. An idea can materialize while you experience a particularly pink sunrise, taking in your own emotional response and wanting your character to experience the same reactions.

Be Alert.

It isn't enough to see a man walking his dog. See the details. Observe. How does the man walk? What kind of dog is he walking? How does the dog behave and how does the man react to the dog's behavior? How does the man behave and how does the dog react to the man's behavior?

Take Action.

Ask yourself, "How can I use this in my current work?" Regardless of the answer, write your observations down. If you can't use them immediately, file them away—you may need them for a future scene or project.

Practicing these three A's will enrich your writing, bringing you fresh ideas, and adding real-life details to your writing. Enjoy!

Madelyn Bello wrote her first story in grade school and has been writing ever since. She has completed two fantasy romance novels and is working on her first contemporary paranormal story. For further information on adding vividness to your writing, check out www.madelynbello.com.

Rhetorical Devices: Powering Up with Style
By Margie Lawson

What are rhetorical devices? A rhetorical device is the use of language that creates a literary effect.

Why should fiction writers use rhetorical devices? They are stylistic ways to grab the reader's attention. They increase a writer's options to add power. They speak to the unconscious of the reader.

Most fiction writers use the same four to six rhetorical devices. Their list may include alliteration, metaphor, oxymoron, rhetorical questions, simile, and the oh-so-fun onomatopoeia. Those first five are common. You may remember the sixth one, onomatopoeia, which refers to words that imitate the sounds they denote: Buzz. Murmur. Click. Thrump. Glug. Pitooie. Pffft.

A small percentage of authors expand their rhetorical repertoire to give their readers a fresh read. They use obscure rhetorical devices that often play off the repetition of words and phrases. I teach writers how to use more than 25 rhetorical devices to add psychological emphasis to their writing. Anaphora is a favorite. We'll zoom in on anaphora.

Anaphora is repeating a word or phrase at the beginning of three or four successive clauses or sentences. The first three are always in a row. If there is a fourth repetition, it's usually one sentence or several sentences later and is most effective as the last sentence of the paragraph or as a standalone line in the next paragraph. Several *New York Times* bestselling authors use anaphora to empower opening chapters as well as their turning points. Lisa Gardner often uses anaphora at turning points in her work. Here's an empowered paragraph from *The Survivor's Club*. Lisa Gardner gave us two back-to-back examples of anaphora in one paragraph.

> But her whole body was shivering, trembling, quaking. And she couldn't stop thinking about her empty bedroom. She couldn't stop thinking about that one bedroom window. She couldn't stop thinking that she would swear, she would swear, she would swear that Dead Eddie had been standing right there.

You can feel the energy in that example. The rhythm. The echo. The repetition of the message. Here's an example of anaphora from Lisa Gardner's 2007 release, *Hide*:

But still we ran. As if I could be fast enough to escape the past. As if I could be strong enough to face my fears. As if through sheer force of will I could block Dori's grave from my mind.

Harlan Coben is another *New York Times* bestselling author who frequently uses anaphora. In his 2007 release, *The Woods*, he uses it on the first page of his prologue, as well as throughout the book. Here's an example from his prologue:

I have never seen my father cry before—not when his own father died, not when my mother ran off and left us, not even when he first heard about my sister, Camille.

Harlan Coben spoke to the reader's unconscious with the smooth, three-part repetition of anaphora: not when, not when, not even when. He also slipped in powerful slivers of backstory in that one easy-on-the-ears sentence.

When should you use rhetorical devices? When you want to emphasize a point, emphasize a thought, emphasize a feeling. Use rhetorical devices to pick up pace, to add interest, to jump-start tension in first chapters and to make any scene more compelling. Have fun integrating a variety of rhetorical devices in your fiction. Your work will hook the reader with psychological power.

Margie Lawson merges her two worlds, psychology and writing, by analyzing writing craft as well as the psyche of the writer. She teaches two editing courses online: "Deep Editing: The EDITS System, Rhetorical Devices, and More," and "Empowering Characters' Emotions." She also presents full-day master classes internationally. For more information, you're invited to visit her website, www.MargieLawson.com.

Seven Tips for Sizzling Scenes
By Kate Moore

Good writers learn to think and write in scenes. Scenes engage readers, give a story immediacy, and allow the writer to control his/her pace. Two of the world's bestselling writers—J.K. Rowling and Dan Brown—know the value of a great scene. Here are seven tactics you can use to develop the habit of thinking and writing in scenes.

A lot of writing, like cooking or house painting, is prep work. To write a great scene, assemble the ingredients of a great scene: opposing characters, POV, a great setting, conflict, an irrevocable event, a climactic structure, and the seed of the next scene. Maybe you need to kick your story off with a murder, a discovery, a cry for help, or an accident. Maybe you need to raise the stakes for your characters. Maybe you need to deliver the emotional connection your readers have been waiting for. Each of those story demands requires a scene. A minimum preparation for a great scene would be to list those items. Even better would be to play with each of them to explore ways to make the scene more intense, more sensual, funnier.

You might choose to assemble your scene ingredients in the sketchiest way possible on an index card or a Post-It®, or you might need to fill pages of notes before you begin. Once you are ready to write, consider these strategies:

Anchor your scene in time and space with an opening sentence about someone doing something somewhere. Your writing is not a scene until you do this.

The spy looked up as three strangers entered the Swan.

George Bagby had to stand on a stool to get a glimpse of her.

At quarter to six in the morning Stephanie heard the doorknob to her bedroom turn.

Winston picked his way up the lane through dappled light and shade, stepping out into pools of gold wherever the boughs parted.

Bel put down her fork.

Till Elizabeth entered the drawing room at Netherfield, and looked in vain for Mr. Wickham among the cluster of red coats assembled there, a doubt of his being present had never occurred to her.

Note that each of the sentences above, from five words to thirty-four words, establishes a POV character taking action in a specific place. There is action, not much description. The spy looks at the strangers in a tavern. George glimpses a woman. Stephanie hears the doorknob turn. Winston picks his way into the woods. Bel puts down a fork at a dinner table. Elizabeth enters a drawing room. That sentence is your signal to the reader that a scene is about to unfold. In contrast, the following sentences are narrative summary:

Everyone knew that the two girls were the light of Ed Stafford's life.

Mr. Collins was not a sensible man, and the deficiency of Nature had been but little assisted by education or society.

For ten days after Harriet's departure, Aunt Louisa and the Professor went about their business unconcerned over her whereabouts.

In those sentences, people don't take action. We aren't in anyone's POV. The author is telling his/her readers about the circumstances of the story, and they don't mind for the moment. The information is important, but it doesn't deliver the gut-punch of direct experience. Narrative summary allows the reader to catch her breath, but she only gets a slight pause, not long enough to go back to her bill paying or that engaging conversation with a telemarketer. You want the next scene to come soon. You want to keep the reader up all night.

Set opposing forces in conflict.

Think about how your characters oppose each other in this scene, usually over a small goal. Post-It® notes are a writer's best friend for this element of scene development. Pick a color for each character. Let each Post-It® represent an action the character takes to reach his goal or to block the other character from reaching his/hers. Screenwriters call these elements the "beats" of the scene. Your job is to break the big conflict into these small pieces and assemble them in an ascending order of intensity.

Give your scene a three-part structure.

Three is the number of wholeness in art. Three trees make a row. Consider these famous threes: three little pigs; three bears; three billy goats gruff; three ghosts in *A Christmas Carol*; three balls in Cinderella; three battles for *Beowulf*. In the opening of *The Mayor of Casterbridge*, Michael Henchard offers to sell his wife three times. When Mole is lost in the wild wood, three sets of enemies pursue him. Art has form. The right form convinces the reader; lack of form leads to static or jumping conflict.

You might want your scene to be a wild ride, but consider the popularity of the roller coaster in all its forms. The coaster is a carefully structured ride—the steep ascent with the creaking car, the first plunge, the wild twists and turns, and the climactic, almost airborne moment. What does the passenger want to do after she climbs out of the car? She wants to ride again. The experience is not random; it is carefully crafted to create those thrills. Structure your scene so the reader gets a great ride.

Most scenes depend on dialogue. Never let your characters agree.

The two most famous love scenes in literature are the two balcony scenes from Romeo and Juliet that frame the whole of the relationship between the lovers. Every line of their dialogue expresses conflict.

"It is the lark."
"It is a nightingale that pierced the fearful hollow of thine ear."

Whenever these two reach agreement on any point, Shakespeare introduces a new conflict. Jane Austen uses the same technique. When her characters do agree, or agree to desist, she switches to narrative summary, but quickly introduces a new conflict.

Write your scene twice (at least).

Write as if you are the POV character with all the thoughts and observations he/she has. Then write as if you are the non-POV character and all you can do is express yourself with body language. Get up; act out your part; show what you feel. What are you doing with your face and body as the action and dialogue unfold? Write your actions into the scene where they occur.

Focus your scene on an irrevocable event.

Lisa Gardner tells the story of learning to write her big books by ruthlessly cutting scenes in which nothing happens. In your scenes, make sure that someone dies, divorces, marries, makes love for the first time, betrays a friend, tells a lie, learns the truth, loses everything, or sacrifices everything. If your heroine and hero have great banter over coffee, lose the coffee and move the great dialogue to a chase, a stakeout, or a funeral. If Harry Potter is tried in London by a court of the Ministry of Magic, but they acquit, lose the scene. Actually, if you are writing anything that good and that successful, do whatever you want.

Plant the seed of the next confrontation between your protagonists.

You don't need to write narrative summary ever if your characters let the reader know when and where they will meet next. This is the "Beam me up, Scotty" technique. How do you get your characters from this moment to a moment two hours, days, or weeks later? You mention that next meeting, and then write a sentence from Step 1, and you are there.

As you apply each of these strategies, you make the choices that distinguish your voice and your book. In a recent workshop, agent Kelly Harms of the Rotrosen Agency advised writers to reexamine ordinary choices to find the extraordinary. Her recipe for a bigger book was: make a list of the big points in your story, and change every one of them.

Kate Moore is a Golden Heart winner and two-time RITA Award finalist, a mom, a full-time teacher, and a Library Journal Top Pick for both her Regency historical and contemporary romances. She blogs with the Fog City Divas at www.fogcitydivas.com.

Less is More: Eliminate unnecessary words that weaken your writing

By Kay Keppler

No one ever sat down to work on a manuscript and said, "Tonight I'll delete 400 words."

No one says that, but excising fluff should be part of every writer's vocabulary. Deleting words, phrases, sentences, paragraphs, even (oh, no!) chapters, is the easiest way to sharpen your storyline and emphasize your themes.

Of course, you don't want to put your cursor in the middle of your page and press the Delete key until your finger cramps. How do you decide what should go? Ask yourself: Does the word or phrase serve its purpose? Must it be there? If you were putting it on trial in a courtroom, does it make its case?

Every editor has a list of words and phrases for which they search and destroy. My list includes actually, really, very, in order, there is/are, a variety of, a number of, and because of the fact that. Not only are these words unnecessary, they pad your writing, diluting its effectiveness. If your sentence reads, There are a variety of cases in which pets make good companions, see how much stronger it becomes if you write, Pets make good companions.

Almost every word that ends in -ly should be deleted. Find a stronger verb instead. (So—instead of walked slowly, use dragged or slouched.) Almost every sentence that starts with It should be rewritten—unless you're Charles Dickens and you just wrote, It was the best of times, it was the worst of times. Recast verb phrases that include not (for example, replace did not remember with forgot).

If you're not sure that your paragraph, section, or chapter is working, delete it. Put it in a separate file with your other orphans and see if, the next time you read your manuscript, you miss that section. Maybe it belongs someplace else. Maybe it belongs on the cutting room floor. But if you're not sure that it works, you can be sure that it doesn't.

Will Strunk said it first, and it's still true: "Vigorous writing is concise. Your sentences don't have to be short, but every word has to count."

Kay Keppler has been an editor of nonfiction and fiction for 30 years. Her first illustrated novella, "Sweet Seduction," was published by MyRomanceStory.com. Her second novella appeared in June 2007.

Researching and Writing an Historical Romance
By Clare Langley-Hawthorne

Writing an historical romance involves finding a delicate balance between history and storyline. Although historical research is essential, it should not overwhelm or overburden the critical aspect of telling an engaging story that involves strong characters as well as plot. I am often asked how I conduct and incorporate my historical research, and I always preface my answer by saying that, no matter the time period I am writing about, the story itself must always remain paramount. It is easy, however, to get swallowed up in the minutiae of research and to feel a strong urge to use as much of it as possible in the story (either to prove you've done the research or because the research reveals such interesting tidbits that you just don't want to leave any of it out). At this point I step back and evaluate the role of history in the story I am telling.

History provides a unique backdrop to the story. It can provide a wonderful sensory transportation — taking readers back in time so they can see, smell, and hear what it must have been like to live in the past. The historical time period also provides an important framework within which the characters must operate — their conduct, manner, and thoughts must be consistent with the era yet also accessible to modern-day readers. In addition, the time period imposes obvious constraints on the relationship between the key protagonists (no sex before marriage for women in Victorian England, for example — well, none that anyone found out about). So before setting out on my research I consider each of the following issues.

- The timeline (month by month, day by day) for my story. What key events do I want to incorporate, or that provide a hook for my story? How can I ground my reader in time and place through using these events as well as the season or activities of that time? For example, I may want to explore a relationship in Ireland against the backdrop of the 1916 Easter Uprising — that particular event therefore provides a critical element to the story.

- The outline. How can I identify the critical plot points for the story and ensure that these are believable for the time period? I wouldn't have an unchaperoned meeting, for example, if that would not have been socially acceptable at the time unless it could be justified in some other way.

- The research items I need to explore to enhance this story (make it richer, more textured and more inviting to readers).

These usually center around the daily lives of the characters, so I know I need to research:

- Transportation. How would my characters have traveled? What would they have been able to afford to do? How long would it have taken them? How would they have traveled (accompanied by servants, or chaperoned)?
- Clothing. What would my characters have worn (and how would their clothes reveal something about their social class and personality) on the outside and underneath? It's always very frustrating to read an historical romance that gets the underwear totally wrong!
- Conversation. How would my characters have spoken? What accent or dialect would they have used? What words or slang would have been in common usage? What words would not have been used? This is always a tricky issue as the story still needs to be accessible to modern readers and sometimes too much historical accuracy in dialogue can sound stilted or may even be incomprehensible.
- Social conventions. What would and would not have been socially acceptable? What were the moral standards and strictures of the day? How did people behave within the context of the historical period? An English duke in the 18th century is hardly likely to hang out at the local pub with his tenant farmers.
- Arts and entertainment. What was the music, literature, and arts scene at the time? What would my characters have been talking about? What were the popular forms of entertainment?
- Politics and society. What was the political and social environment for my characters? How did this impact their lives?

This list provides a brief overview of the principal areas I consider, but I never research these in isolation—I try always to consider how my story will unfold, what my character's motivations are, and then let these guide how I structure my research so that I won't find myself drowning in too many historical details.

The Internet provides a terrific resource for any type of historical research, but be warned: not all of it will be accurate or unbiased. I always like to turn to scholarly, well researched secondary materials to get an overview of the period. There are also many good books that provide a starting point for looking at daily life, such as Daniel Pool's *What Jane Austen Ate and Charles Dickens Knew: From Fox Hunting to Whist — The Facts of Daily Life in Nineteenth-Century England*. I subscribe to an online library (Questia) which I use to find material, and I visit libraries (here in the U.S. and in the U.K.) to access both secondary and primary sources. I have found magazines, newspapers, and books written at the time to be invaluable sources of information about daily life. They also provide details about clothing, turns of phrase, and social conventions at the time.

I think the best way to approach historical research for a romance novel is to imagine that you are looking at the period through your characters' eyes: what do they see, hear, smell, and feel? How do they view the world around them? How would they really behave?

Once you have this perspective, it becomes easier to cast off the details that do not add to your story. This can be a fine balance — too many historical details and your story will drag, too few and it will lack texture and depth. Let the story and your characters be your guide, and never feel the urge to tell the reader all that you have discovered in your research.

Finally, I have a good rule of thumb: If, on my second or third reading, an historical fact or detail pulls me out of the story, I edit or delete it. Similarly, if I find myself doing research for the sake of research and losing sight of my story, I stop and go back to focusing on writing rather than researching.

Clare Langley-Hawthorne was raised in England and Australia. She was an attorney in Melbourne before moving to the United States, where she began her career as a writer. Her first novel, *Consequences of Sin*, was published in February 2007, and is the first in an Edwardian mystery series featuring the Oxford graduate, heiress, and militant suffragette, Ursula Marlow. The second book in the series, *The Serpent and the Scorpion*, is an August 2008 release.

The Efficient Writer: Research with Ease
By Madelyn Bello

Create more time to write by making other parts of your writing life more efficient. The following are a few research tips.

1. Use TiVo®. Use the keyword search function in TiVo to find and record shows for you. When I wanted more information about the Philippines, I set TiVo to record all relevant shows for me to watch later.

2. Use Google™. I use Google.com for two purposes: to find websites with the information I need and to mine all the news stories, sending to my inbox any articles regarding my research topic.

3. Search it. Browse the online library databases for reference material. I use the local library's online database and search for books that I'm interested in. I request that the materials be sent to the closest library branch for me to pick up at my convenience.

4. Scan it. Tired of transcribing notes from a research book? Invest in a personal scanner (some come as small as the size of a pen) to scan pages from a book and transfer the information to your computer.

5. Hire help. Let kids or friends help with your research. Have them read or watch shows and talk with you about what they learned. If something sounds interesting, you can go back to that source yourself.

6. Use RSS. There is a lot of information on the Internet, and we all have our favorite websites and blogs that we like to frequent. But what we don't have is a lot of time to keep checking to see if new material has been added. Sign up for an RSS Reader and have the information come to you.

Madelyn Bello wrote her first story in grade school and has been writing ever since. She has completed two fantasy romance novels and is working on her first contemporary paranormal story. For more tips on creating more time to write, check out the expanded article, and other resources, at www.madelynbello.com.

PART III
CONNECTION

"Copyright law protects your exclusive right to exploit (use productively) your original work. Copyright law was written to encourage the free exchange of ideas and to stimulate the progress of 'useful arts,' which benefit society. The theory behind the law is that the progress of useful arts is in the best interest of society but that creative individuals will not freely share their work without some say over how it is used."

-- *Literary Law Guide for Authors: Copyright, Trademark, and Contracts in Plain Language, Second Edition* by Tonya Maria Evans

Wild Card Goals and Career Success

By Margie Lawson

What is a Wild Card Goal? It's big. Perhaps seemingly unachievable. At one point it was a dream. Your dream. A dream you'd like to achieve. A Wild Card Goal may be a goal that at one time seemed so far out of your reality that you couldn't fathom reaching it. Depending on where you are in your writing career, your Wild Card Goals may be anything from querying your first manuscript to publishing your fiftieth. From interviewing a *New York Times* bestseller to getting on the *New York Times* bestseller list.

Perhaps it's a goal you can control, but haven't chosen to control. Perhaps it's a goal outside of your control, yet one you can influence. The beauty of Wild Card Goals is that they help you create your career map. You do have a career map . . . right? Without a map, how do you know what you could do to get where you want to go?

Here's one way you could create your career map:

- Use a large piece of paper. Flip-chart paper is ideal.
- In the lower left corner, put a big symbol indicating "you are here."
- In the upper right corner, put a big symbol indicating your destination.
- Write your Wild Card Goals (1, 2, or 3) and your reality-based goals at or near your destination.

What steps could you take to reach your goals? Free associate! Fill your page with real possibilities and off-the-wall ideas. Those ideas may include spin-offs from the following:

- Writing the book, completing the book
- Networking in your local writing groups and across the world
- Self-promotion, from headshot to website to writing articles
- Volunteering, small dose or big dose, it all counts
- Self-image, from confidence to dressing the part
- Growth, sharpening all your saws—from writing craft to pitching to professional book signings
- The business of writing—taxes, contracts, marketing

You're brainstorming. Stretching possibilities. Keep in mind that writing down ideas does not commit you to them. You do not have to follow up on all of your amazing ideas. Next, add your best-guess time line to each idea where a time line could apply.

Back to creating your flexible career plan on that big piece of paper:

- Draw mind-mapping branches that shoot off from your career path.
- Put the main ideas on your career path, with offshoots for the spinoff ideas. Use colored pens.
- Do not strive for art. Strive to create a career map that will help you see what you could do to achieve your goals.
- Keep your map out where you can see it.
- Revise or recreate every few months to update your career map.

Now I'm asking you to do something that may seem difficult. Rein in those big dreams. Think smaller. What are the small things you can accomplish? Get them on your map.

What if you don't come near achieving your Wild Card Goals? Can you set yourself up for happiness no matter how far you go? We're all going through our lives as best we can. What really counts? Family. Friends. Health. Happiness. Living a good life.

As a psychologist, it's important to me to help people go as far as they can go in pursuing their life dreams. Sometimes life interferes. Make your map. Reach for your dreams. Psychologically take care of yourself along the way. Think big, and enjoy every career success.

Margie Lawson merges her two worlds, psychology and writing, by analyzing writing craft as well as the psyche of the writer. She teaches online courses, including Defeat Self-Defeating Behaviors, and presents full-day master classes internationally. Please visit her website at: www.MargieLawson.com.

Mentors and Professional Organizations Can Benefit Your Career

By Elizabeth Edwards

What would it be like to learn to paint from Picasso? Or learn to invest from Warren Buffet? Can you imagine having Oprah teach you how to build a media empire? How quickly would your career take off if you knew what Danielle Steel knows? These people might be a little too busy to take your call, but there are successful people all around us you can learn from.

No one who's successful got there on her own. The biggest problem with going it alone is that you have to make a lot of mistakes. This simply takes too much time. Having a mentor can help you avoid many of the time-wasting, enthusiasm-depleting mistakes that lead to inertia.

One saying I like goes like this: "If you want what I've got, do what I do." The point is that success isn't a secret. If you adopt the mindset and copy the behavior of a successful person, chances are good that you will experience similar success. When we have the opportunity to benefit from the experience of someone who has gone before and figured out what works and, more importantly, what doesn't work, we gain momentum. There is a big difference between knowing what to do and doing what you know, so accountability is major plus.

A mentor is more than a model. Mentors provide feedback and networking opportunities. They can be the source of important constructive criticism and become your biggest cheerleader. Finding the right mentor is key, so find one that has accomplished what you are working toward. Additionally, your mentor should have good communication skills, honesty, and a willingness to help you. Why would someone want to help you? Most successful people love to share — and chances are that your mentor had a mentor, too.

I suggest that you start by finding someone who can encourage or mentor you. You might be surprised how quickly you find people who want to help you. My second suggestion is to join professional organizations such as the Romance Writers of America. Once you get involved, you'll meet people who know people, who know people. It is the six degrees of separation, the law of attraction in action. The key: you have to show up and get involved.

Elizabeth Edwards is a native of Northern California, lives in the San Francisco Bay Area and writes historical romance and time-travel romance novels. She is a singer/songwriter and is actively employed in the recording industry.

Pitch to Your Niche: Discovering Your Strengths
By Shelley Bates

Remember that game at the fairgrounds with all the little buckets mounted on a board? The purpose was to get a ball into one of those buckets. Sure, if you took a handful of balls and tossed them all at the board, some of them would be bound to score. But what if you were told that, once you'd tossed your ball in a bucket, you could only throw to that one for the rest of your playing time—no matter what bucket you were aiming at in the beginning?

The publishing industry is like that. If you sell a book, they're going to want you to write more books like it for the same market. So, if you've got a Regency historical, a chick lit, and an inspirational lined up as your next projects, the publisher is not going to want any of them if you've just sold them a hot series romance.

If your heart is really in the Regency era, writing two Blazes a year for the next three or four years to establish your name and gain a readership is not going to make you happy. You might get frustrated and cranky, and your heroine will start to snipe at her hero and you're going to have to write your way out of love scenes that start with her telling him she has a headache. Your editor will take a look at your numbers and decide you're not as good an investment as you used to be, and then where are you? Starting over in the historical market four years later with a new name, no experience, and no track record.

So, look at the market, at your own strengths, and then carefully and know-ledgeably choose where you will invest the bulk of your time and talent. Be smart, be analytical, and be brave. Throwing spaghetti against the wall is easy. Control-ling where you want your career to go is scary—but it's important to your career to pitch to your niche.

There are two ways to analyze your strengths: internally and externally (yes, GMC --goal, motivation, conflict--comes into everything). Let's look at the internal elements first.

Reading taste: Each of us loves to read certain kinds of books. Not only did I love gothics, I spent eight years with the Royal Canadian Mounted Police soaking up narcotics investigations and homicides. So when I started writing, I gravitated naturally to romantic suspense. Six rejected manuscripts later, I concluded that what I liked to read was not the same as what I was good at. Shirley Jump (*Really Something*, Zebra, 12/07) wrote several unsuccessful suspense manuscripts, too, and then tried comedy almost by accident. "It was like putting on the right pair of shoes—all of a sudden, I was writing exactly what I was meant to write," she says.

Voice: This is a mysterious thing that writers more experienced than I have spent a lot of time trying to define. There are sometimes three or four workshops on this alone at the national conferences. If you're looking for some help with voice, listen to Julie Elizabeth Leto's tape from New York, or attend one of Barbara Samuels's workshops. If you're familiar with your voice, it's a good tool to help you find out where to pitch your work.

Writing process: Does it take you two years of agonizing labor to complete a manuscript, or do you write a book in an obsessive frenzy in six weeks? Are you as prolific and disciplined as Nora or Suzanne Brockmann, or are you like Jenny Crusie, who says she sometimes waits years for the girls in the basement to send up workable material? If you're a fast writer, category may be a good niche for you. If you're slow, aim for a single title publisher who will want one book a year. In her article, "Juggling Books and Publishers," Julie Kenner says, "For a lot of authors, that first book is the baby you slaved over, spent months or even years polishing. Now it's sold, and suddenly you can go to contract with the next book on proposal. Unless you've been paying real attention to your writing habits — how long you need to have an idea gel; how many pages you can produce daily; if you simply must do multiple drafts of a book, or if you edit as you go; and if you can get back into a story after being lost in another for days — then you're going to have a difficult time when the publisher comes back and wants two or three books from you, and then asks you for input on spacing your deadlines."

Manuscript length: If all your manuscripts are three inches thick and you have an entire bookcase full of research binders, you probably shouldn't be writing for Harlequin Presents at 55,000 words. If, no matter how hard you try, you can't squeeze a word out past 60,000, don't submit to a single-title house whose minimum is 90,000. Instead, look at some of the Harlequin lines, the Kensington or Avon anthologies, or the novellas from Red Sage and Ellora's Cave, and pitch to them.

Subgenre: Ann Roth (*The Pilot's Woman*, Harlequin American, 3/08) says, "I think many writers have the same problem I did: They want to write one kind of book but their voice and style fit better elsewhere. I truly believe that is why some of the very good writers out there can't seem to sell." You may be able to write suspense, inspirationals, and social comedy, but remember, when you're choosing your niche, think long-term. Where is the greatest source of your contentment and inspiration as a writer? In what subgenre do most of your ideas fall? Choose to set your career path there.

The second way to discover your strengths is external input. Your critique group, a contest judge, and especially a rejection letter from an editor or agent are all excellent sources of information. Yes, it sucks when we get a rejection or a low score. But after the emotion has passed and we've gained five pounds from all the consolation chocolate, we can analyze rejection letters and contest critiques to see where they can help us. That's what they're for.

Rejection letters: Don't let the fact that your work has been declined blind you to the clues in the letter that may be helpful to your career. Pam Toth, who has more than 30 books published, says that editors don't toss off compliments just to be nice. If you get a personal letter instead of a form rejection, you're being treated as a professional. If the editor wants to see something else from you, it means that she likes your writing. If she makes specific suggestions and asks to see the book again, she sees something promising in it but feels that it needs some changes. She may also be testing you to see if you'd be easy to work with or a prima donna. Pam adds, "Too many times I've heard writers say that as soon as they read 'I'm sorry, but this doesn't work for me,' they stopped reading." They never realize that an invitation to submit something else is in the final paragraph. I had fifteen rejection letters for *Grounds to Believe* when I was targeting it to the ABA (American Booksellers Association) market. See if you can pick out the clue I should have seen in this comment: "The strong focus on the religion competes too much with the romance. That said, I do believe you are very gifted, and I'd be delighted to read something a little more to the heart of the market from you anytime." I finally saw the problem. Instead of cutting down the religious part, I bumped it up to a whole new level and sent it to the CBA (Christian Booksellers Association) market. I queried Steeple Hill and six days later got a letter requesting the complete. Two months later they bought it—and two years later it won a RITA Award. A liability in one market can be exactly what another market is looking for.

Critique groups: Another source for external input is the critique group. Alisa Kwitney (*Token*, 2008) was in Columbia University's fiction writing program trying to write serious literary fiction. In her spare time, she'd jot down little snippets that were light and satirical to entertain her classmates. She says, "It took about six months to realize that my fun writing was being received well and my serious writing was being poked with lots of pointy objects. So I decided to make my snarky, talking-to-friends tone my official voice, and discovered that my strength was in being funny." Being true to her writing strength has paid off. *The Dominant Blonde* was featured in *Publisher's Weekly* and excerpted in *Cosmopolitan*.

Contests: Ann Roth is a firm believer in contests to help you discover where your strengths are. She says, "Say you want to write a single title romantic suspense. You enter the first chapter of your novel in a contest. The judges say your story is not a suspense, it's a sweet romance. This could be a clue that you're working toward the wrong line." Or, three judges all have the same comment about your pacing. Maybe you should focus your revisions on this area instead of tweaking the dialogue for the umpteenth time.

Money: When you're pitching to a publisher, it's tempting to read Brenda Hiatt's "Show Me The Money" chart (www.brendahiatt.com/id2.html), find out who pays the most, and start there. Money can certainly play into your decision to send your material to one publisher versus another. So can the fairness of their contract, or how much of their marketing budget they're prepared to devote to a debut author. But money should not be the determining factor. If you're a suspense writer, don't lock yourself into the erotica market just because it's paying well at the moment. Think of money as merely another piece of data on which to base your decision about the niche where you fit best. And don't quit your day job.

In publishing, you have to start somewhere. Why not make it the place where you're most comfortable and can shine? You'll succeed because you laid the groundwork. You took a careful look at yourself and your writing, your style, your habits, and you pitched your book to the publisher who best suited that style and those habits. And when that publisher calls to offer you a contract, you'll be on your way to a happy, long-term career.

RITA Award–winning author Shelley Bates holds an M.A. in Writing Popular Fiction from Seton Hill University, and is published by FaithWords, Steeple Hill, and Harlequin. Between books, Shelley loves traveling, creating period costumes, and catering to her flock of rescue chickens.

The Ins and Outs of E-Publishing
By Doreen DeSalvo

Electronic publishing has exploded in recent years. Many e-pubbed authors have moved from electronic publishing to New York deals; others enjoy fantastic careers strictly in the electronic market. But how do you decide if e-publishing is for you? And once you've decided, how do you choose the right publisher and create a successful e-career? For an inside view of e-publishing from someone who's been there, read on.

Why consider an e-publisher?
Just about every author wants a paper book to hold in her hands, like a trophy that proclaims her a published author. But there are plenty of times when e-publishing is a better choice for an author.

- *When your book is stranger than a palm tree on Mt. Everest.* E-publishers blaze new trails. Remember when New York wouldn't touch erotic romance? E-pubs were there first. The same is true for vampires, shapeshifters, and ménage à trois. Currently male/male romance, yaoi, and manga are hot in the e-pub world. E-publishers have the ability to respond quickly to new trends. They're looking for cutting-edge books, the radical romances that traditional print publishers are afraid to touch. If you're bucking the mainstream trends, look into an e-publisher.

- *When you want a personal touch.* E-publishing can give you a more friendly environment than you'll find at most NY publishing companies. How often will your questions be answered by the CEO of a NY house? Because e-pubs are smaller, you'll get more personal attention.

- *When you're almost—but not quite—ready for New York.* You'll also get more attention when it comes to revisions. This varies from e-pub to e-pub, but most e-publishers have the time to invest in helping you hone your writing. Editors will work with you one-on-one to craft the best book possible, and you'll learn a lot in the process.

- *For the money.* You may not get a large advance for an e-book, but you'll be paid much more promptly than you would from a New York publisher. Most e-pubs pay royalties every month. You'll also enjoy a larger royalty percentage, typically 35 percent or higher.

- *When you crave instant gratification.* Okay, "instant" is a bit of an exaggeration. Even so, most e-publishers will release your book much more quickly than a New York publisher. If time-to-publish is particularly important to you, ask the publisher how far in advance they're scheduled. Like NY publishers, some e-publishers have a huge backlog of titles in the queue, and yours might not see the light of day for a long time. You'll also be pleasantly surprised by how much fan mail you receive. E-book customers are voracious readers, and they love telling authors how much they enjoy their books.

Not all e-pubs are created equal.

Before signing on with an e-publisher, evaluate the company. Make sure to ask the following questions before you commit.

- *How long has the company been in business?* You'll probably sell more copies with a company that's been around for a while. An established e-publisher has a wider readership than one that's just opened its doors.

- *How many titles does the company release each week?* There's a balance between too many and too few releases. Too few releases may mean that the publisher is new on the block or has a questionable reputation with authors. Even if the company is solid, readers only revisit sites that frequently offer fresh new titles. In contrast, some e-publishers release too many titles. With too many new titles, readers become jaded and will often postpone a buying decision, thinking, "No hurry . . . I can wait to see what's new tomorrow before I buy." Chances are you'll do best with a company that releases a regular number of new titles every week, because readers visit the site when they know there are new releases on a regular basis.

- *Does the company ever promote old titles?* On most e-publishing sites, your book will fall off the home page after less than a month. Some companies make an effort to promote older titles by cross-selling them on the home page if a new release is similar in theme or genre to the older books. Also, take a look at what happens when you add an e-book to your shopping cart. You should see a "You might also like these other titles" message. That tells you the company is serious about cross-selling your book when a similar book is ordered.

- *What are the contract terms?* Generally speaking, e-publishing contract terms are more favorable to the author and more negotiable than New York contracts. But be warned: If the publisher gives you verbal assurances about contract terms, make sure to have those clarifications written into the actual contract. Some e-publishers' contracts ask for all rights, and the term is often longer than reasonable. The majority of e-book sales are earned within the first year or two, so why sign a long-term contract if the sales will slow to a trickle for the remainder of the contract? Try to get the term shortened whenever possible. In a similar vein, why give the publisher film, video, and other subsidiary rights if they're never going to use them?

- *Are there any rumors flying around about this company?* Sure, every author has a different experience with her publisher, and the blogosphere is rife with snarky rumors. But if you hear that a company bounced a royalty check, threatened to sue an author, or reneged on contract terms, proceed with caution.

- *Does the publisher want books like mine?* Just like a New York house, each e-publisher has their own criteria for what they're publishing. Check the guidelines, and only query the ones who publish what you have to offer them.

Maximize your online sales.
Your work as an author doesn't end when your book hits the virtual shelves. A large part of your success will be determined by the efforts you put into your electronic career.

- *Publish often.* When you have a print book on the shelves, all readers interested in romance will see your book side by side with every other publisher's offerings. But with an e-publisher, readers have to come to the publisher's website in order to find your book. It can take two or even three books at one publisher before the readers who habitually visit that company's site start buying your books in large numbers.

- *Get out there and chat!* There are hundreds of e-mail loops, blogs and bulletin boards devoted to e-book romance. While following all the buzz can be a major time waster, make sure you're chatting often enough to let readers get to know you. Note the word chatting. Nothing turns a reader off faster than an author who only posts promotional news or contest announcements. Keep your posts brief if you must, but pick a few loops and participate in them frequently.

- *Sex sells.* The best-selling books in e-publishing are erotic romance. Why is this? Perhaps it's because a lot of readers don't want to have steamy print books lying around the house. E-books are stored on the computer, where they're easier to keep private. Generally speaking, the more your book sizzles with no-holds-barred sex, the more readers will flock to purchase it.

- *Keep in touch with your editor.* E-publishing editors know the ropes just like any NY editor. Ask your editor for help in making your books hit the mark. What writing strengths can you develop and build on? Where could you make improvements? Your editor knows your writing intimately, and she has insight into the industry that you might not.

- *Be professional.* E-publishing is a small world. Editors frequently move from company to company, and corporate mergers happen. If you decide to leave one company for another, do your best to leave on good terms. To ensure you have the best options in the future, always keep your side of the street clean.

Breaking out of e-publishing into a successful New York career happens—witness the success of MaryJanice Davidson, whose *Undead and Unwed* was a wildly popular e-book before being picked up by the wise people at Berkley. But there are hundreds of other authors who have successful careers solely in the e-publishing world. Whether you decide to stick with online publishing or branch out into wider realms, e-publishing can be a valuable part of your career.

Doreen DeSalvo has been published—electronically and otherwise—for more than 10 years. Since 2004, she's been the Chief Financial Officer of Loose Id Publishing. You can find her steamiest books at www.loose-id.com.

Writing a Query Letter
By Allison Brennan

Writing a quality, professional query letter may make the difference between getting an agent to read your manuscript and a form rejection. But writing a query is a far different process than writing a book—a skill you would be wise to learn.

It's not impossible. Think of it as a business letter where you're talking about something you have passion about: your book. Professional yes, but not so formal that you distance yourself from the reader (agent) and make your book sound boring. Enthusiasm is wonderful and you should show that excitement in your letter.

Here's a tried-and-true formula for writing a query. Good luck!

Elements of a query letter
All query letters should have five key elements:

1. *Intro.* Why are you querying that agent? Because they represent your genre? They represent a specific author your work is similar to? You met them at a conference and they indicated interest? Tell them how you pulled their name out of the hat.

2. *Hook.* In 25 words or less, what is the hook, the high concept, the "wow" of the book?

3. *Summary of your book, like a back-cover blurb.* In fact, read dozens of back-cover blurbs and you'll find they have a certain rhythm and feeling. Design your summary as you would if you wrote the back-cover blurb. You want to hook the agent. You can include a summary ending, but this is a query—you don't have to give away all your secrets.

4. *Hint at the audience, either by comparing your tone to that of other authors or by showing what audience would be interested in your book.* For example, "TITLE is a 100,000-word romantic suspense that would appeal to readers of A, B, and C." Or, "TITLE is a 100,000-word historical suspense that blends the historic richness of X with the cutting-edge suspense of Y and the sexy romance of Z." Basically, one sentence that tells who would buy the book.

5. *Personal information about yourself, including any awards, publishing history, memberships.*

And do all of this on one page. I, personally, like the block letter style for business letters. This means no indents and an extra return between paragraphs. Part of what I learned about marketing through letters I learned in my former career. I wrote constituent mail for the California State Assembly. People don't want a lot of wordy, technical garbage. They want answers. But if you use lofty words or long paragraphs, their eyes glaze over. They're busy. Likewise, when I wrote memos to legislators about an idea for an outreach program, I had to keep it to one page—and simple. They're not stupid (well, most of them aren't), they're simply busy and pulled in several different directions at once. If I want them to use my idea, I need to show them it will work—quickly.

Agents are the same way. They have hundreds of queries to read every week—why should they request your manuscript? Give them the reason by hooking them with your query. You should spend the time developing your query letter because that's your first impression. Even if you met the agent/editor at a conference (and definitely reference that in your letter), you need to draft a professional query.

Self-analysis
Review your latest query letter.

- Do you have a hook? (My hook was "Ex-FBI Agent turned crime fiction writer wakes up to discover someone is using her books as blueprints for murder.")
- Did you summarize your book in three paragraphs or less? Does it read like a back-cover blurb? Consider that most back-cover blurbs are 5–8 well-written and well-designed sentences. Would your blurblike summary make you want to buy the book? (Or make you request the full manuscript if you were an agent?)
- Do you include personal information, including phone number, address, and e-mail?
- Is it one page, in a 12-point readable font? Does it look like a professional business letter?

Some reasons to target agents over editors:

- So many of the big houses accept agented-only material.
- Good agents know the market and keep up on the trends.
- Good agents know the editors—often personally—and who is buying what.
- Good agents know how to pitch editors and get them to read a manuscript faster.

- Good agents understand contracts and can negotiate a better deal for their authors. This isn't just about money. It's about rights and options and the fine print.
- An agent is your buffer between the editor and you. You can focus on writing and working with your editor on making a good book great; your agent can focus on negotiations in all aspects of your career—from the contract, to what the publisher is going to do on publicity, to making sure you're getting paid on time. In essence, an agent is your pit bull. Your advocate. They know when to fight and when to let go.
- Finally, a good agent will help you build your career. They won't be afraid to tell you something is sub-par, or that something is exceptional. They'll help you slow down, speed up, or whatever it is you need to do to keep your career moving forward.

How to create and target your agent list.

Compile an agent list for your genre. Some ways to build the list include finding out which agents represent authors who write in your genre, or who are seeking material in your genre, even if they don't currently have an author. Find them through their online client list, the acknowledgement pages in current books (most authors, especially debut authors, thank their agent), and search PublishersMarketplace.com and the archives of Yahoo loop messages. Buy *Writers Digest*, and pull from there as well as just asking other writers. Agentquery.com is another good resource.

Now, cull the list. Are these agents making recent deals? Look at their authors—that's usually a good indication of whether they are consistently selling, especially if they don't report to PublishersMarketplace.com. Karen Fox (karenafox.com) has a list of romance specific deals and who represented them. Verify all the information you find off the Predators and Editors website (www.anotherealm.com/prededitors/pubagent.htm), as well as Writers Beware (www.sfwa.org/beware/agents.html).

Once you pull out all the bad agents or those who aren't representing your genre, start asking. You shouldn't blanket query, but have "prequalified" all your agents. Meaning, they are reputable, don't charge fees, and either have recent sales or are a new agent in an established agency.

Prioritize your agent list—which may be 40, 50, 100 agents—into an A, B, and C list. The criteria is however you make it—i.e., what's important to you—but the way I did it was my A list were agents with top agencies or a top agent on her own, but who had at least one bestseller in my genre. B list agents were new agents in top agencies or solid selling agents on their own. C list agents were reputable, but either newer agents with only a handful of sales, or established, selling agents with no breakthrough clients. You may want to factor in location, or references (you have a friend with the agent) or something else (like an agent you met at conference and you clicked with may go to the top of the list.)

Start with the A list. Why not? Dream big. Then work your way down. But the most important thing to remember is that rejection isn't personal. It's business. So keep writing new and better books, and keep querying. All it takes is one yes.

Allison Brennan is the *New York Times* bestselling author of eight romantic thrillers. Her current book is *Tempting Evil*; *Sudden Death* is available in October. She lives in Northern California with her husband and five kids.

What an Agent is Really Looking For:
Another perspective to consider
By Scott Eagan, Agent, Greyhaus Literary Agency

The scene is always the same. Sometime during a conference, there will be a room full of writers sitting and staring at a table full of editors and agents. The writers should be tapping into these individuals who may potentially be the key to their success. Inevitably, one writer will stand up and ask an agent that one question that they believe will be the key to unlocking the mystery of getting published.

"So, what is it that you look for in a piece of writing?"

Wrong! Wrong! Wrong!

The answer this writer is likely to hear is the same one every writer has heard time and time again: "I'm looking for a great story, with great characters that really stick with me." Or, "I'm looking for a story that I simply can't put down at the end of the day."

While the answer is not as specific as a writer hopes it to be, it is the answer that matches the question they asked. Unfortunately, that answer gets the writer no closer to being signed by an agent or advancing their career toward publishing.

The problem is, the writer has asked the wrong question. The goal, then, is to know exactly what the right question is, especially in the case of finding an agent. So, to determine what that correct question truly is, it is important to stop and examine the unique relationship between an author and an agent. It is important to really know what goes on when an author and agent finally begin working together.

The agent/author relationship.

To begin with, although an agent begins looking at an author through that single piece of writing she has submitted, this is just the tip of the iceberg. The relationship goes far beyond the simple (although it is far from simple) task of selling that manuscript.

The relationship between an author and agent is teamwork. This means that the agent and the author have to know that they can work with each other, and to work together for a long period of time. Remember that the agent is in this for the long haul. This is for two reasons: First of all, the agent is in this relationship to help the author build their career. This is not simply the project of putting one book on the shelf, but the process of building a readership and making that author a household name. This, of course, leads to the second point. The agent will only make money if the author sells books, and this will not happen with the first book.

In most cases, the money does not come pouring in on that first book; it will be a book much later down the road.

For this reason, the agent wants to make sure that they have an author that they can work with.

What an agent is really looking for.

Returning to that conference and the writer's initial question to the agent, the real question should be, "What do you look for in a writer, beyond the story?"

Asking this question really gets to the heart of the issue. Because this is an interpersonal relationship, there has to be a great chemistry between the agent and the author. The answer lies in four basic areas the agent is looking for in an author:

- The author's knowledge of the market.
- Does that author know their place?
- Can the author show a commitment to the team?
- Is this someone we like?

Let's look at each.

The author's knowledge of the market.

The writer has to understand how the market works and their place in this world. Writers who are successful at the Greyhaus Literary Agency know how long the process really takes for a manuscript to get published. They understand that their book will not be an overnight success, and that the odds of earning a six-figure deal on that first book are slim to none, especially in the romance industry.

Caren Johnson of the Caren Johnson Literary Agency also notes that when she looks for new writers, she wants a writer "who treats writing as a business." This means that she wants a writer who, if they write romance, hasn't simply heard of the genre. They are well read in the genre and "know how to make a reader sit up and take notice."

Having an agent does not mean the writer should be ignorant of the business. The writer needs to know her fair share.

Does that author know their place?

This idea really works with the knowledge of the market element. A writer needs to have a true sense of reality when it comes to their place in the marketing world. All writers would love to have their book on the New York Times bestseller list, but in all reality, this is not going to happen.

One of the biggest turn-offs at the Greyhaus Literary Agency is the writer who comes in believing that her book is far better than that of the established writers. In fact, one author actually stated during a pitch session at a conference that they knew they were better than Nora Roberts and they planned on taking her down hard. While the writer may be a great writer, coming in with that attitude was a sure sign that she would not be added to the list. Confidence is great. Cockiness is not.

Can the author show a commitment to the team?

Remember, this a team situation. Writers need to be clear that there is much more going on in the agency beyond simply their story and their agent. This means that they do what they can to assist the other writers in the agency, promote the agency, and most importantly, work closely with the agent.

At the Greyhaus Literary Agency, writers realize that there are other writers and, at times, their stories take precedence over their own work. This may be due to upcoming deadlines for a given writer, or specific contractual situations that arise that put a current work in progress of another author on hold.

Caren Johnson goes on to add that the "hardest thing for a writer to hear is that there is only one agent and usually 30 or so authors." It would be great to have 100 percent attention all of the time with every author, but there is simply not enough time in the day.

Is this someone we like?

Look, there are some people who just do not get along with other people. If a writer is one of those people that only does well working with their computer, then finding that agent is going to be a tough task. Simply put, an agent has to like the author. If the agent finds the author needy, or bossy, or if the agent finds the writer someone who is just plain difficult to work with, there will be no motivation to push for her book.

Both the Caren Johnson Literary Agency and the Greyhaus Literary Agency have much the same approach to writers of this nature. It is a big turn-off when a writer believes we work for them. Caren Johnson describes this type of author as someone that has the attitude of "get my manuscript to this person." Remember, that the author has signed with an agent because of his or her knowledge of the business. They did not sign with this person to act as their personal mail carrier.

Although writing is a solitary life, being a professional writer is very public and the editors, readers, and general public have to like the writer as a person.

So now what?

For those writers who have led themselves to believe that it was only the story that mattered, they might wish to sit back and consider what they have been doing to get that agent. If they have a drawer full of rejections, it might not be because of the writing. It may simply be because of the way they approached the agent.

This does not mean that an agent will sign a writer because they like them. The story still plays a huge role in this decision-making process. Just remember that there is more to this decision than, "I'm looking for a great story, with great characters that really stick with me." Or, "I'm looking for a story that I simply can't put down at the end of the day."

Scott Eagan has been an agent with the Greyhaus Literary Agency, located in the Pacific Northwest, since 2003. Scott has sold to Pocket, Sourcebooks, Dorchester, Avalon, Harlequin, Mills and Boon, and other major New York publishers.

The Secret To Picking Up Extra Editor and Agent Appointments at National
By Judy Sabel Soifer

Here is my sad story with a happy ending: Last year I attended Romance Writers of America's (RWA) national conference in Dallas, and I missed my editor and agent appointments on Friday because I had written them down as being on Saturday. In my horror, thinking all sorts of things—like I'd be banned for life by RWA from ever getting another editor or agent appointment—I went to the appointments check-in desk to plead my case and found out how understanding the people at RWA are. I got new appointments, and I also found out how one can pick up extra appointments, even if you didn't miss yours.

When I went to the appointment check-in desk, there were 20 to 30 people waiting to pick up an extra appointment, or hoping to get an appointment because they didn't get one in the mad computer rush to begin with. The number of attendees waiting for first or additional appointments was hard to determine because they were grouped with those waiting for their scheduled appointments. As the appointment times came up, the woman in charge would announce the editor or agent's name and say if there was an open spot. You would think that there would have been a mad rush for each opening, but there wasn't. What I realized was that each editor and agent was looking for a particular genre and that each person waiting for an appointment wasn't competing for the same appointments. As for what happened to me, the woman in charge came over to me and quietly told me she had an opening with an agent who was looking for what I wrote.

After the conference, I contacted the agent and editor I had the missed appointments with. Both were very understanding, saying people make mistakes and not to worry.

I had heard that you could pick up an appointment at National, but I didn't know you could pick up extra appointments. And I didn't realize how few people actually do this. So if you've missed your appointments for whatever reason, or you didn't get an appointment to begin with—you might still be able to schedule one onsite. Going to any conference can be a bit stressful as well as exciting. If you make a mistake, knowing you won't be banned for life by RWA can help lower the stress and make Nationals fun.

 Judy Sabel Soifer, writing as J.M. Sabel, is an ex-ballerina who hung up her dancing shoes to work with children in the field of nursing. She has a master's degree in pediatric nursing. She's a writer and illustrator working toward publication. For more information on Judy, go to her site: web.mac.com/jmsabelsoifer.

Four Important Tips When Working with Agents —And if You're Lucky, a Publisher

By Josie Brown

So you've written a novel. Welcome to the club! It's a big one, too: According to Bowker, the media barcode registrar, more than 172,000 books were published in 2005. Of these, close to 80,000 were novels. And just think: That doesn't even include those authors who, like you, have yet to find a publisher for their manuscripts!

Does this sound discouraging? It shouldn't. That is, not if you've chosen writing novels as your profession as opposed to your hobby. In fact, like any business startup, it should be a welcomed, exhilarating challenge.

As the ad slogan goes, "Membership has its privileges." But in regard to this nebulous organization I'll call the Novelists' Club, the truth is this: Privileges for an author are earned, and most often, as a result of longevity. And in this business, longevity comes with book sales.

The way we live now, a novelist can't be a hobbyist who doesn't care about creating a name for herself. The hobbyist certainly doesn't have the nerve to send out her manuscript to agents who may not like it, or who may actually love it, and (best case scenario) sell it.

The professional novelist, on the other hand, realizes that reading is a subjective process, and that she will get rejections from several agents on her wish list. But that's okay, because there will also be one or more who love it and see the author as an emerging voice whom they would be proud to represent. Now, here are some tips that will make you a lifetime member of the Novelists' Club.

Tip #1: Choose your agent wisely.

Literary agents, who get paid commissions of fifteen percent upon the sale of their clients' books, must be astute in choosing the kind of manuscripts they feel editors will buy. In that regard, not all agents know all editors. In fact, not all agents know, or sell, to all publishing houses, or for that matter sell both fiction and nonfiction. For that reason alone, your wish list should include agents that do sell fiction, and more specifically, the kind of fiction that you like to write. If your book is, say, historical romance, but an agent on your list doesn't know or sell to romance publishers, then that agent should not be on your list in the first place.

And while a good agent knows more than just a few editors at a limited number of publishing houses, great agents stay connected with a couple of editors at each imprint at many publishing houses, specifically those editors who are senior enough to make sure that their clients get due consideration beyond the actual editing and production process, to the promotion and selling of the book.

Tip #2: Trust your agent's judgment on the editing changes.

In the publishing world of today, the literary agent plays a vital role: He separates the literary wheat from the slush pile chaff. You can believe that your agent has seen other manuscripts get rejected for voice or plot issues similar to the ones he questions in your story. And he certainly has his finger on the pulse of what is selling now, and what may have sold last month but is now considered passé in the fickle world of publishing. He cannot afford to tell you only what you want to hear, because if an agent consistently sends editors books that they don't feel merit their attention, he will soon lose those editors' consideration.

So yes, listen to your agent. It is in your financial interest to do so.

Tip #3: Review a list of potential publishers and editors with your agent.

Your agent should have an idea of where your book fits in that heavenly firmament of publishing houses. However, you too should have your finger on the pulse of your marketplace, and feel free to pass along any info that you feel may help make a sale. That said, do your homework on recent deals made for books in the genre you write (mystery, suspense, sci-fi, contemporary romance, historical romance, literary historical, the list goes on and on). A good place to start is an online subscription to either PublishersMarketplace.com or *Publishers Weekly*, where you can scour recent deals and the editors with whom they were made. Joining a writers' organization, such as Romance Writers of America, puts other resources and networking contacts at your fingertips.

Tip #4: Choose your editor carefully.

A best-case scenario is that more than one editor loves your book, and is interested in putting up money to acquire its rights.

That said, if your book does have the good fortune to go to auction, the imprint with the highest bid may not necessarily be the right deal for you in the long run. Why? Because your best bet is to go with an editor who loves your voice enough that she is willing to go to bat for you beyond the editorial process for this book, and subsequent ones—and that may not be the editor with the biggest budget.

The best editor for you is one who pushes and inspires you to hone your story. She will invite your suggestions for the cover and for the plot description copy on the back cover. Ideally, she is a cheerleader for your book to her editorial director and to the sales department so that your book is given its fair share of promotional consideration. Best yet, she pushes for it to be a "lead" book (one of the few books launched in any given month or season that garners strong promotion with the major bookstore chains).

All of these criteria should be important to you and to your agent in building your brand. (Yes, as an author, you are a brand, and don't you forget it!) In fact, these points should be included in the negotiation process for your book contract. You may not get everything you want (most first-time authors don't). But if the editor truly wants to be in business with you, then she will hear your concerns and work with you in addressing them up front, so that your book has an honest chance to succeed financially, for both you and your publisher.

And you—a professional novelist who has worked long and hard to reach what in truth is just the starting line—deserve nothing less.

Josie Brown's glam lit novels are *Impossibly Tongue-Tied* (Avon) and *True Hollywood Lies* (Avon). You can read her books at her blog: www.josiebrown.com and email her at JosieBrownAuthor@yahoo.com.

View from the Verge

By Karen Morison-Knox

The chasm between unpublished and published stretches before you. You stand on the verge, finished manuscript in hand. Contest judges and critique partners assure you that your book will sell. Each submission could be the one that results in The Call. Every cell in your body tingles with anticipation. You wait. And wait.

Friends and family ask, "When are we going to see your book in the store?" Still you wait, only now you are grinding your teeth.

Welcome to the verge.

I've been on the verge so long, there have been times I've wished someone would shove me over the edge and end my misery. But I've also used the time to move my career forward and to prepare for when The Call does come. There are many things you can do:

- **Enter contests.** Be selective. Enter contests where the final judges are agents or editors who specialize in your subgenre. The feedback will help you hone your skills, and every time you final, you add another credit to your resume. I attracted my first agent solely on my three First Place contest wins.

- **Start your next manuscript.** Editors want authors who can produce. Get a jumpstart. Think of Nora Roberts and her magic drawer of finished manuscripts. When an editor asks, "What else have you written?" you'll be ready.

- **Volunteer.** Volunteering gets your name and face known. Author Liz Maverick chauffeured out-of-town editors and agents when they came to speak at her chapter meetings. She recognized a unique opportunity to have private, face-to-face time with people who could enhance her career.

- **Seek RWA's PRO status.** Look on the organization's website for details. PRO status affords you preferential agent and editor appointment sign-ups at the national conference.

- **Learn.** Hone your craft. Attend seminars on book contracts, creating a brand, building a website, and publicizing your book.

The verge can be maddening. By using the time wisely, you'll boost that leap to the published side.

Karen Morison-Knox is a freelance editor and an award-winning, yet-to-be published author of paranormal romance and middle-grade fantasy.

The Author/Agent Relationship:
Communication Begins with Your Joint Contract
By Elaine English and Tawny Weber

From the author.

Communication is key in any relationship—none more so than one between an author and agent. Especially since signing with or changing agents is a major career move. It can be great, or it can severely derail your career and confidence. The difference often comes down to how well the author and agent are able to . . . you got it, communicate.

One of the key things you as an author can do is know ahead of time what you want and need in an agent. If you're clear on your priorities and career goals and do your research, you can work toward finding specific agents who fit those needs. More important, you can communicate that information during negotiations. Agents aren't mind readers, and they might not have the same vision for your career as you do, so it's crucial to make sure you're both on the same page before you enter a partnership.

Once you've narrowed your agent choices, many authors agree that if possible, you're better off meeting the agent in person. Conferences and RWA chapters offer many opportunities for this. But even if it's only by phone, spend time really talking with your potential agent. Ask yourself how comfortable you are. Do you feel like you're really communicating? Are you on the same page as far as career vision and goals are concerned? And if not, do you feel like the agent is listening to what you have to say with an open mind? Do you see this person guiding your career? Keep in mind that you're not looking for a new pal or best friend. You're looking for a career partner: someone with the knowledge and experience to help you achieve your career goals.

I'm a strong believer in the power of an agent. They can make you bigger deals, snag better advances, and can guide your career from fledgling to blockbuster. Even though I write category, I still wanted an agent in my corner, especially one who was an expert on contracts. Your very first collaboration will be the contract that binds you. My agent, Elaine English, is both an agent and a literary attorney, which gives her a very savvy handle on the particulars of contracts. When asked what writers should look for when signing with an agent, here's what she said.

From the agent.

If you are going to be an author, you'll definitely need to know about contracts. You may, at times, work with other writers or editors and will need to outline the responsibilities and rights of each. You may seek representation of a literary agent. If so, there needs to be some understanding of the terms of that relationship. And of course, the holy grail is that publishing contract. So no matter how much you'd prefer to just sit in front of your computer with your muse in overdrive, you'll need to take a few minutes to understand at least the basics of contracts.

A contract is nothing more than an agreement between two or more parties. It sets out the rights and responsibilities of each and the consideration that makes the deal binding. Contracts can be oral, i.e., reached as a result of telephone or in-person conversations. In most cases, these are just as binding as written agreements. Contracts can also be entered into seriatim, i.e., in a series of email where there is a back-and-forth exchange and agreement of terms.

There can be problems, however, with verifying the precise terms agreed upon in each of the above examples. Too often, parties to oral agreements suffer memory lapses and later, when called upon, deny that essential terms were actually part of the bargain. Email contracts can also get sloppy, unless each email addresses each and every point under discussion.

So, in my view, the safest way to proceed when you're making an agreement with someone that you want to be binding is to put it in writing. No special formalities, i.e., notaries, are required in most cases, just the signature of all parties acknowledging they have read and agreed upon all the terms as stated. The Author's Guild suggests it is better for authors to have oral contracts with their literary agents because they are easier to terminate. The Guild's position is that later if the agent wants to enforce something, i.e., a commission on unsold books, the burden will be on the agent to prove you had agreed. However, the reverse is also true. Should the author need to try to enforce something, e.g., how quickly payments are forwarded, the author will also suffer the problem of the wavering memory defense.

In this short piece, there's not enough time to really cover the specifics of agent and publishing contracts in any detail. An introduction to important concepts and terms will have to suffice.

In any contract with an agent, there are a few absolute essentials: what will be represented (only one book or everything you write); what will be the agent's commission (both percentages and reimbursement for expenses); how soon will the author get paid (needs to be detailed if you want to hold the agent to a timeframe after receiving your money from the publisher); what is the agent's authority to bind the author to agreements with others (publishers); and when, how, and under what terms can the relationship be terminated.

For those of you who don't know, publishers typically pay authors through their agents. This means your check will come first to the agent, who then deducts his agreed-upon fees and sends the remainder on to you. It is essential to clarify payment terms so there's a clear understanding of when and what you'll get paid.

Defining the authority of the agent can be important to avoid later problems. When the agent says "OK" to an editor, are you formally bound to that deal, even when at that point you may not have even heard the terms? As an author, you want it clear you have final approval over any deal and that only your signature on a dotted line will legally bind you to an agreement.

The parting of an agent and author is rarely a pretty scene, but it can be much less painful for all concerned if the procedure is already outlined in a contract. I can attest from many years of personal experience that it's better to hammer out those details at the beginning of the relationship when things are positive and both parties are thinking clearly. Once a problem has arisen and emotions come into play, sorting things out becomes much more difficult.

An essential to always remember is that the publishing contract is drafted by the publisher and, therefore, is intended to protect the publisher's interests first and foremost. If you want to make sure your interests as an author are protected, then you need to understand the contract, and perhaps, negotiate for some changes. There are business terms in the publishing agreement, i.e., what rights are being licensed and what money you'll get for them, as well as legal issues such as warranties and provisions holding the publisher harmless against claims. There are typically noncompete concerns (critical, if you hope to write for more than one publisher at a time), ownership of characters, and option issues.

If you're concerned that your agent may not have considered all the technical legal aspects of a publishing contract as well as you'd like, you can always consider having an attorney who specializes in publishing law review your contract as well. Even if you don't understand every word, it's important for you to review the document and ask your agent or attorney to explain any provision you don't understand. Remember, it's your name at the bottom and you are the one who will be bound by its terms. Whether you're signing with your first agent, or looking to make a change, read the contract carefully and clarify any points you're not sure of. If there's anything you don't feel comfortable with, discuss it with the agent and find a way to correct the issue.

Take your time. After all, this is your career. You want to talk it through and make sure this is the right agent for you.

Three-time Golden Heart finalist Tawny Weber dreams up stories in her California home, surrounded by dogs, cats, and kids. Her latest book, Does *She Dare?* is a January 2008 Blaze. She loves to hear from readers—visit her at www.TawnyWeber.com.

Elaine P. English is an attorney and literary agent in Washington, D.C. She advises her clients on matters involving contracts, copyright, trademark, libel, privacy, and other issues relating to publishing. She handles only commercial fiction, including women's fiction, romances, mysteries, and thrillers. See her website at www.elaineenglish.com.

What To Expect When You're Expecting . . . A Book
By Kalen Hughes

One of the big shocks I suffered after I sold was the sudden dearth of information out there about just what happens next. What was I supposed to be doing? What pitfalls should I be aware of? How could I avoid them? Just what is the logical progression of things? I'm going to lay out my experience here (along with a few insights from watching my friends go through the same thing) in the hope that this information will help you when your time comes.

Once the euphoria of "The Call" wears off, reality hits: Writing has just become a J-O-B, complete with deadlines, responsibilities, and maybe even a crazy boss. Expect a brief span of time when your brain simply refuses to function, especially if you've made the sale sans agent. I went from ecstatic to frantic about two minutes after the end of The Call. For 48 hours I was paralyzed (good thing The Call had come at the end of the week).

If you're now looking for an agent to handle the contract, be prepared for the fact that not all agents will be willing to take you on, even under such wonderful circumstances. And respect them all the more for it. The agent who said no to me said it for perfectly valid reasons (she just doesn't "get" my voice).

The very first thing that's likely to happen is a title change. There are a variety of reasons for this. In my case, my editor loved my title, but Marketing/Sales didn't. Out it went. My friends and I (with the help of a few bottles of wine) brainstormed a list of potential new titles. I whittled it down to fifteen options and sent them off . . . Marketing/Sales came up with their own title. Guess which one stuck?

Lesson number one: You can't win an argument with Marketing.

Don't even bother trying. These people can make or break you, and you want them to be on your side. Plus, they know what they're doing. If they say The Confessions of a Baby-Eating Greek Sheik will sell, trust them.

Lesson number two: Revisions suck, but everyone has to do them at some point.

Get over it and do them. Some people sell, and the book is bought and published "as is." Lucky them. Maybe. An editor has a keen eye for what works and what doesn't, so if your editor requests revisions, take her request seriously. I know my book is far stronger because of my editor's input, and many—if not all—of my friends say the same of their own work.

Expect to hit a wall when your book turns into what the Divine Nora calls a POS (piece of sh*t). Most authors I know hit this a day or two before their revisions are due. Just keep breathing and keep working. The feeling passes. I promise.

Depending on what house you're with, there will be some kind of cover consult right about now. At the very least, you'll be asked to fill out a sheet with some basic information (hair color of protagonists, setting, and so forth). If you're a very, very lucky girl, maybe you'll get to show them covers you love and suggest that you'd be over the moon if they got "hunky model du jour" for your cover. A girl can dream . . .

Something else to figure into the equation is that if you sell to a print publisher, you're likely to have a multi-book deal, which means you'll need to be working on these future books while you're going through the initial process of getting book one from manuscript to shelf. You're no longer juggling a single ball, you're now one of the Flying Karamazov Brothers, trying to keep a bowling ball, a flaming torch, and a running chainsaw in motion.

Your cover arrives via e-mail. It's the moment of truth. Love it or hate it, you're probably stuck with it. The art department has done their best. They've presented multiple options to Marketing and your editor, and they've probably had some kind of knock-down-drag-out about which one to go with. Expect your cover to surprise you. It may be a good surprise, or it may not. But be prepared to find a way to make yourself love it, 'cause odds are, as a new author you're stuck with whatever they give you. Try to remember that your publisher's goal really is to sell as many copies of your book as possible, not to let it die on the shelf.

Lesson number three: Learn to love your cover.

You'll probably have similar ones for your next few books as your publisher seeks to "brand" you. See Lesson One.

Somewhere in here you start worrying about getting a cover quote from someone whose fame is intimidating. Your agent and/or editor will help with this, but it's still nerve-wracking. The angst as you fret that they won't like your book enough to offer a quote is excruciating, but survivable. Remember that in our neck of the woods, authors want to help each other.

Intermingled with all of this is all the nonwriting promotional stuff you need to be doing: Creating a website if you don't already have one, blogging (either your own, or establishing a presence on other peoples' blogs, or both), setting up your Amazon Connect account, attending conferences, teaching workshops, being active on reader loops, and so on. It's exhausting, and a huge time suck, but there's no escape. For the newbie author, it's promote or die.

Lesson number four: Promotion matters.

It may not be trackable. It may not be tangible. But it matters to your publisher (and probably to your agent) that you're putting yourself out there. It's a matter of good faith.

Expect to put in a lot of long hours on your website, blogs, loops, and other channels. This is just part and parcel of being a published author nowadays. Go on the offensive and make sure that the romance community knows who you are and what you have to offer them (and try to make sure that you really do have something more to offer than just your books). I'd also advise that you really become a member of the loops and blogs, not just a drive-by promoter. Readers can smell insincere self-promotion from a mile away.

Now you get book two off to your editor! Wheeeeeeeee! Euphoria envelops you all over again. Then, of course, revisions for book two arrive at the same time as copyedits for book one (and don't forget that you need to be working up a proposal—or two or three—for book three).

Lesson number five: Expect tight deadlines.

You need to be ready to turn around your copyedits or the galley in a matter of days. This can be a little scary, especially if you happen to be—I don't know—out of the country. Yes, I was in Morocco when my galley arrived. Another lesson to jot down: Sometimes no matter what precautions you take, things will go sideways. Just do the best you can.

Copyedits can be a nightmare if you get the wrong copyeditor. Some will try to change your voice. Some will take issue with fact that you like em-dashes or ellipses. Some will flag things as erroneous when they're not, or will change/challenge a word they don't understand. You have to consider each and every change and stet those that you disagree with.

This is also the last place where you can make any substantive changes. Did you find out that you got a medical or historical term wrong between turning the book in and receiving the copyedits? Change it now. Did you realize you need to emphasize a point that you let slip? Fix it now! Need to change a name, hair color, delete a secondary character? Do it now!

Lesson number six: Choose your battles carefully.

Don't argue with every comma change. Try and remember that the copyeditor is your friend. They're trying to help you (even if all that ink spilled on the page makes you want to curl up and die).

Once the copyedits are done (and yes, those take priority over everything else), get back to the revisions for book two. Get them out of the way ASAP so you can get back to the proposals for your next book (or to working on book three if you've already sold it).

If you're lucky—and aren't we all—your galley for book one will show up at the same time as your copyedits for book two. Yes, I'm being sarcastic. The galley is your last chance to catch typos and things of that nature. Any change you make at this stage costs your publisher money. Correct anything and everything that's not your fault (typos, missing words) but be careful about any other changes. You're usually limited to how many you can make, so make very sure that you know what your publisher allows at this stage. Regardless, don't suddenly decide that the hero should have been blond!

Go over your galley with a fine-toothed comb and then send it back in as quickly as you can (most houses give you five to seven days for this review).

Right about now it's time to get an excerpt up on your website and link to Amazon so people can preorder your book (it'll most likely be up there six to eight months out).

Lesson number seven: Timeliness is professional.

You want your editor to love you. You want to get a gold star. Turn this kind of stuff around quickly. And if there's a reason it'll be delayed, tell your agent or editor. If someone dies or is diagnosed with leukemia, tell someone. It's better for them to know what's going on than to think you're simply slacking off.

Somewhere in here you may or may not get Advance Reading Copies (ARCs). Not all publishers give ARCs to authors. If you get them, make sure and send copies to some prominent reviewers (whom your publisher is not targeting) and to the WaldenBooks Romance Experts (you can get the addresses for these ladies from Sue Grimshaw, the romance buyer for Borders).

You might want to consider making your own ARCs and sending them out to select web reviewers. It's not that hard and a few well-placed reviews can only help. Have bookmarks or postcards printed up with your cover on them. Hand them out. To everyone. Set up interviews with reader blogs. Think about running a contest. Dig down and start focusing on promotion.

Order "signed by the author" stickers.

Start establishing your Amazon presence. Do a few plogs (the Amazon version of a blog). If you have a short story gathering dust, think about using it for the Amazon Shorts program (but only if it's your best work and closely resembles the voice and setting of your first book; there's no point in posting a crummy sci-fi short if you're trying to sell your historical romance, or vice-versa).

Plan a party for your book launch (you deserve one!). Better yet? Get your friends and family to plan it for you.

Lesson number eight: Don't forget to stop and savor your accomplishment.

Kalen Hughes was born and raised in Northern California. She grew up participating in a wide variety of historical reenactment clubs, giving her an unusually personal perspective on history that she hopes brings added verisimilitude to her writing. An active costume historian, she has taught creative writing, horseback riding. Currently, she lives in the San Francisco Bay Area with an ancient pit bull terrier, and can often be found writing in one of the many local coffee shops. For more about her and her books, check out her site at kalenhughes.com.

Building Buzz: Word-of-Mouth Marketing

By Jacqueline C. Yau

Once you've written your masterpiece, whether it's your first or your twentieth book, you need to let your readers know that your book is hitting the shelves. How do you build a viral marketing campaign to spread the word? Here are ten ideas.

1. **Build a sticky website.** Provide fresh content so readers keep coming back. Think of ways to leverage and link the content on your site to engage your reader. What do they want to know about you? Take a look at the websites of your favorite authors. What information do they share on their sites? What else would you want to know about them? Apply that to your own site.

2. **Bust out your uniqueness.** Build your brand. What makes your voice and book distinct from the other offerings available? What promise are you making to the reader each time they read your book?

3. **Develop an elevator pitch.** Share what you write in the time it would take you to have a short conversation in an elevator. Punctuate your pitch with action verbs and key phrases to hook the listener and cover genre + hero + heroine + villain + 2nd act journey (through the dark moment).

4. **Roll out a loyalty program.** Provide a tangible benefit for loyalty. Do this, get that. For instance, readers who provide their e-mail addresses get special access like advanced previews, downloads, online chats with you, and are entered to win a personalized love note from the hero.

5. **Create community.** Provide a forum for your readers to connect. Authors like Christine Feehan, Jennifer Crusie, and Sherrilyn Kenyon are pros at this.

6. **Deputize your own buzz agents.** For your extra-loyal readers who are connectors, like reviewers and bloggers, feed them behind-the-scenes tidbits that they can spread for you.

7. **Network, network, network.** Conferences, reader groups, and online loops are great places to connect with potential readers.

8. **Listen to your readers.** Get ideas from your fans. They often have the best suggestions.

9. **Send out bite-sized chunks.** Provide teaser excerpts and short interviews with characters.

10 **Create a cause.** Perhaps you have a favorite charity? Leverage that cause for PR, i.e., for every book sold off your site, donate five percent of the proceeds to that cause.

Jacqueline Yau has sprinkled her marketing fairy dust in organizations large and small, including Nestlé USA, Wild Planet Toys, Hawaii Public Radio, and TiVo. When not waving her wand, she's writing romantic adventures.

Branding Basics: The Brand Called You!

By Jacqueline Yau

What do J.K. Rowling, iPod®, Nora Roberts, Target®, and Google™ have in common? They are all powerful brands that conjure powerful associations in our minds. These are not merely products. If that were the case, I would buy any brand of toilet paper—but I buy Charmin® toilet paper. I want all of the cushiony, quilted softness the company promises me if I buy it.

What is a brand? It's a promise from you, the author (the producer of the product) to your customers of the specific benefits, quality, and value that your product (your book) will provide them. It is a perceived, subjective association that adds value beyond the basic product function (i.e., to provide a story). A brand is timeless, whereas a product can be imitated and is generic.

Your readers associate you with a certain payoff whenever they read your book. Think about your favorite authors. What associations come to your mind when you think of them? For instance, Christine Feehan is known for her powerful paranormal romances featuring alpha males and strong yet innocent heroines, with lush sex scenes.

How do you define your own brand and build it? First, ask yourself the following:

- What subgenre(s) in romance do I write?
- What's my voice? Is it light? Dark?
- What themes do I explore most often? Beauty and the beast? Redemption?
- What can my reader expect every time they read one of my books? Great plotting? Dynamic dialogue? A military alpha hero? A heroine afraid of intimacy? Innovative sex scenes?

Next, determine how you want to represent your brand in graphics, fonts, symbols, and color. What elements make your brand recognizable from others? Candice Hern produces exquisite bookmarks, stick'em pads, and a website that all possess the same look and feel, evoking the Regency England period in which she writes. Ensure that your entire packaging enforces the positioning you've created.

To sell, a well-written novel is imperative. But by also paying attention to building your brand, you will increasingly attract readers who buy on the strength of your name alone.

Jacqueline Yau has sprinkled her marketing fairy dust in organizations large and small, including Nestlé USA, Wild Planet Toys, Hawaii Public Radio, and TiVo. When not waving her wand, she's writing romantic adventures.

The Writer's Challenge: Test Your Promotion I.Q.
By Brenda Novak

TRUE or FALSE?

1. Networking and promotion are a waste of time, especially for a midlist writer. To be successful, all you have to do is write a great book.
False. Networking is integral to most people's success, especially in the current marketplace. Why? It's a mathematical certainty. The whole is always greater than its individual parts. I cannot know everyone or everything. But if I link up with others, who link up with others, who link up with others, we establish the kind of shared knowledge and power that will enable us to achieve more as individuals.

2. I must be good at every aspect of writing and promotion to succeed.
This is equally false. Networking allows for specialization, which increases efficiency. You only have to be especially good at one facet of promotion—so you have something to offer those who are good at others.

3. Networking is about synergistic relationships.
Probably the truest statement here. Studies have shown (not surprisingly) that people act out of self-interest far more than they act out of public virtue. So if you want others to support you, give them the incentive to do so, or work out a trade. Identify key individuals who can make a difference in your career: agent, editor, distributor, bookseller, reviewer, and so on. Decide what it is they need to be successful and give it to them. If you're the real article, they'll have no reason to refuse you representation or the purchase of a manuscript or a great review. You have now switched all those toggle switches normally set at no to yes.

4. As writers, we are selling stories.
False. We have to sell ourselves first and foremost—our ability to entertain. That's why it's so important to build and maintain credibility with everyone we meet each step of the way.

5. Some things are out of our control. We can give it all we've got and still fall short.
False. Some things are out of our control. But we won't fail if we give it all we've got. You might not achieve the goal you want in the timeframe you were hoping, or in the particular manner in which you set out to attain it, but you will only fail if you give up. There are too many opportunities out there to believe

otherwise. If one approach doesn't work, try a new one. Don't be too stubborn to adapt and improvise. There is no shortage of opportunities, only a shortage of time and, even a bigger problem to some, an unwillingness to make the sacrifices necessary to take advantage of those opportunities.

What sacrifices am I talking about? Time and effort. The time to sit down and write a different book or type of book. The time to do market research. The effort to overcome shyness or fear to make the right contacts or get in front of the right people. The effort and determination to overcome rejection. The effort to fight doubt.

It's easier to give up and blame our lack of progress on circumstances beyond our control.

6. You have to have a "platform" to sell a book these days.

False. Platform has become a big buzzword in the industry. It used to be more connected to the nonfiction realm (and probably still is), but it basically means you have to be promotion worthy to begin with (for example, you're already a celebrity, you were kept in a cage as a child and have written your memoirs, you're a credible astronaut who claims to have seen an alien). A platform is something "high concept" or with a hook of its own that helps you gain widespread attention.

A platform is definitely an asset, but it's not absolutely necessary. You can build a platform if you don't already have one. How? Become an expert on some topic. Carve out your niche by doing something noteworthy besides writing a book. Or enter your work in contests that, if you win, will set you apart. Such things give you leverage when dealing with the media, which is the springboard to free publicity.

7. It takes more than being a nice person to be a good networker.

True. It helps to have charm and charisma, but there are plenty of folks who are incredibly nice, yet never seem to get ahead. Why? They're either not capable of writing a compelling book or, if they are, they're not effective at convincing others of their ability to be a marketable commodity.

8. I have to do big things to make a big impact.

False. Anyone who has read Malcolm Gladwell's *The Tipping Point* will tell you how small things can start a social epidemic or create the tipping point we're all hoping for. The Law of the Few (80 percent of the work is done by 20 percent of the people) also shows the power of small. It's better to do key things, smart things, than to try and launch a huge, unfocused promotion campaign. Put some thought into your promotion plans and go after the sector of the market that will be most likely to get excited about your particular style of book—and most likely to share that excitement with their friends and family. You want to recruit others to your cause—the kind of people who will advertise you and your stories for free.

9. It takes a lot of time to network.

Absolutely true. Networking is about maintaining relationships, and maintaining relationships that aren't superficial takes time, true dedication, and effort. But networking can exponentially increase the impact you make in any one industry. (It's also very fulfilling in a way that has nothing to do with reaching professional goals, but this article is about professional success, so I digress...) Make a list of PR goals for the day, week, and month, and set aside the time to accomplish them. Becoming a bestseller depends first and foremost on the quality of the work—but as I'm trying to convey, that isn't always enough. There are a lot of talented writers who have never hit a list or even published a book. The difference is in setting yourself apart, getting above the media noise, and effectively conveying your message, which message is the same whether you're dealing with industry professionals or readers: I won't let you down. Convince enough people of that and you can accomplish anything.

10. Promotion costs too much money for a new writer.

False. There are a lot of things you can do that cost nothing. But, again, it requires a sacrifice of time and effort. You can network. You can write articles. You can send out press releases. You can launch Internet campaigns. You can write a captivating blog. You can create an e-zine that grows your mailing list. You can learn how to create and maintain your own website. You can do speaking engagements, which will help establish you as an expert. You can start a book group. You can do charity work. You can join social clubs. You can advertise your website in the front of your books (most publishers allow this, anyway). You can get creative and do something unique like the Online Whodunit Game that fellow author Karen Rose and I did last summer (www.ucanmodel.com).

Brenda Novak is the national bestselling author of 25 novels. Summer 2008 will see the release of her next three romantic suspense stories—*Trust Me*, *Stop Me*, and *Watch Me*, coming from Mira Books. Visit her website at www.brendanovak.com to learn more about her and her work, or to participate in her annual online auction for diabetes research, which takes place May 1–31.

Reviews: The Good, The Bad and The Ugly
By Regan Taylor

The good news is, your book has been picked up for review. The bad news is, your book has been picked up for review.

What exactly does that mean and why should you have your book reviewed?

Over the past several years, more and more authors have realized the impact of a good review on their books. Concurrent with the increased demand for reviews, more and more review sites have cropped up. Two years ago, industry standard was a 30-day turnaround for a review to be posted. That timeline has moved to about 60 days because of how many books are now submitted to sites for review.

The earliest review sites, such as The Romance Studio, Love Romances (and More) and Fallen Angels Reviews, set the bar for what a review was about, and are still going strong today.

How do you get a review? Ask your publisher if they submit to review sites. Depending on the publishing house, they may only send the hottest titles and authors or they may send out their entire line. If your publisher won't submit your book to the online review sites, and you have a publicist, he or she may send your books for review. Or, you do it yourself. With 30 to 40 main review sites out there, you stand a good chance of having your book picked up for review.

Follow the instructions on the review site's guidelines. Generally, though, expect to send your ARC (Advanced Readers Copy) or book, the back cover blurb, and a 1-2 page synopsis.

Once your book has been picked up for review, treat yourself to some exciting nail biting and teeth gnashing, or just forget it's out there. A word to the wise: Don't write them every couple of weeks to ask where the review is. Don't tell them what other sites are saying. Reviewers are, for the most part, volunteers. They have families, jobs, adventures, and are generally avid readers and dedicated bookaholics. They have an industry deadline (generally 45–60 days) to get the review in. They'll do it.

A good review can make your day, a great one your week. A low-rated one can ruin your month—if you let it. The bottom line, however, is that reviews are really only one person's opinion. So if they are just opinions, why request one? Why take the chance on getting a good one? How do you handle a bad one?

Who will review your book? Reviewers are a mixed lot of individuals. While they are predominantly women, more men are finding their way into the world of reviewing, especially as more science fiction and dark romantic suspense is sent to be reviewed. (Men are also reviewing erotica.) Reviewers vary in background, and country of residence, hence the continued popularity of e-books for reviewing, and age. In response to the growing number of young-adult books available for review, one site recently brought a teen on board to handle that category to ensure that they also receive reviews., They have their likes and dislikes as well as favorite genres, which is why your blurb is so important. While many have their favorite authors and will snap up every new book from those favorites, there are also a growing number who love to sample a new author's work. It's that introductory blurb that attracts a reviewer to your book.

E-books and electronic ARCs are popular to reviewers because, it is easier to search for a name or phrase with the "find" function in Adobe® Acrobat® or Microsoft® Word than to flip through a book and hope it will be found. So no need to wait for a print ARC to request a review. By the same token, don't hold back if you only have print ARCs available.

Make sure you send your ARC with both your back cover blurb and a short synopsis. Review site readers often read the synopsis of a new book to get a feel for a new author's writing and to see if a favorite's latest story is what they are looking for. The synopsis gives you a chance to highlight different aspects of your story. Often a reviewer will be drawn to a thread in the storyline that you may not have thought described the book, but for the reviewer it was a high point of the book, giving your book the opportunity to attract new readers.

So what do you do with the good reviews? The ones that have you grinning ear to ear? Spread the word! Put a quote on your blog and website. Post the review on e-lists and your online groups, and start off an online chat with it. Include a reference in your newest query or, if you are lucky enough to have an advance review copy (ARC) reviewed, include it on your cover. Lastly, note what the reviewer liked, what worked for him or her, and use that as a foundation for what might make your next book just as good if not better.

It's always good business to drop a thank-you note to the reviewer—they'll remember the next time one of your books is available for review. That doesn't mean they will continue to give you high ratings. If they are honest they will tell you and your readers exactly what does and does not work in subsequent books. But you stand a better chance of getting a review. Not only will that reviewer look for your future work, he or she will tell their friends and fellow reviewers. Because ARCs cannot be shared, passed on, or resold, if someone hears about a great read, it can translate into more sales for you.

Not every book is a 5 on a scale of 1 to 5, with 5 being the highest. Not everyone is going to like every book available. Even the most dedicated bookaholic will find the occasional book he or she didn't particularly care for. Yes, a bad review hurts. And can ruin your day. As hard as it may be to believe, a 1 or a 2 rating—and yes, some review sites will post the 1 or 2—isn't personal. It's just that reviewer's opinion. Step outside the hurt feelings and see if there is something you can take away from that review that will help you do better in the future. Use it as a chance to grow.

What shouldn't you do with a bad review?

Don't send a nastygram—they will share it with the rest of their staff. No one will offer to review any of your future books because they don't want to run the risk of receiving the nastygram. Don't tell them that everyone else liked it and don't send quotes from other reviewers. They don't care. It's someone else's opinion; they only care about their own. Don't tell them they must have read someone else's book and they need to get a clue. They know what book they read. They simply didn't like it. Don't ask them to take it down. There are some sites that will only post ratings of 3 and above, sending the 1s and 2s to a recycling bin. Sites that do post them feel that readers are entitled to see the good and the bad so they can make intelligent decisions. Interestingly, there are readers who will look at a lower rated review and buy the book just so they can see if what was said is true.

You can ask for a second reader—maybe the review site will agree, maybe they won't. It will depend on how you ask. Keep in mind, however, that even with a second review, the first one probably will not be taken down.

You can also use that reviewer as the next villain who goes up in flames in your next book!

Good reviews, bad reviews, in the end it's people reading your books!

From reader to reviewer to editor to author, Regan Taylor has seen the good, the bad, and the ugly in books and reviews. She is thrilled that her first western, *Indentured Bride*, will be available in print just in time for the RWA national conference. Visit her on the web at www.regantaylor.com.

What I Know About Publishing
By Barbara Freethy

After 18 years, 26 books, several agents, many editors, and a couple of publishing houses, I've learned a few things about succeeding in the publishing world. Here are some tips I hope you'll find helpful.

The first sale is the beginning, not the end. I remember thinking before I was published that if I could just sell one book, I'd be happy. That would be enough. Well, of course, it wasn't enough. As soon as I'd sold one, I wanted to sell two. But I quickly realized that just selling a book hadn't made me an expert. There were still a lot of things to learn about the business and the craft. And selling another book meant I had to write one.

Avoid the sophomore slump. Refuse to let yourself think that first sale was just a fluke. It wasn't. You're a writer, and not only can you do it again—you will! It's easy to panic on the second book. We often have years to hone that first manuscript, but sometimes the second book is part two of a contract, and you gave the editor only a synopsis of your idea. Now you have to write it and to a deadline. Fear can be paralyzing, but the only sure way to get over that sophomore slump is to write your way over the mountain. Concentrate on writing one page at a time, and put all the fears about whether that second book will be as good as the first one out of your mind, at least until the book is done.

Put yourself in a position to get lucky. Talent, perseverance, and stamina are all traits of a successful writer, but sometimes to make it in publishing you need a little luck. Luck may come at the very beginning of your career—a contest win, a chance meeting with the perfect editor who is dying for a book exactly like yours—or luck may come further down the road. But the only way to ensure you can take advantage of that lucky moment is to be ready. Once you send something out, start writing the next idea. Always have something working for you, no matter where you are in your career.

New editors, new lines, new imprints. Whenever editors come on board, they're eager to build their own list. This can be a great time to get in. Staying on top of what's happening in the industry can put you in a position to get your book on the right editor's desk at the right time.

Don't quit your day job too soon. There is no job security in the world of publishing. At some moments in a career, a writer might feel as if the good could never end—everything is working perfectly, and if you're one of a lucky few, it might stay that way. But many, many writers have careers that resemble roller coasters. Make sure you have enough money to cover the down times.

You're not married to your agent. I can't count the number of times I've heard writers say that an agent/author relationship is like a marriage. This relationship is nothing like marriage. It's a business partnership and should be treated as such. Some agents will be perfect for you at certain points in your career. A few writers will stick with one agent for their entire career, but many others will discover the need to change their representation as time passes. When your instincts tell you that your partnership with your agent is not moving you forward, then it's time to go. It's not personal. It's business.

The one who cares the most about your career is you. A good agent, a fabulous editor, a wonderful publishing house all contribute to your writing success, but no one cares about your career as much as you do. Don't mistake friendship for undying loyalty. Publishing is based on numbers and sometimes editors drop writers they love because of those numbers, just as sometimes authors have to move on to other publishing houses. Nurture your business relationships, but don't put friendship before your career goals.

Don't be afraid to fight for a good cover. It's only one of a thousand covers your publisher is putting out that year, but you'll live with it forever. Even if you lose, it's worth giving it a shot. A bad cover can take years to overcome.

Information is power. Ask questions. Ask for numbers. Print runs with major print publishers are known at least a month ahead of release date, and most of them will give you that information. There are some exceptions, but you won't know until you try. Some authors have been heard saying they're afraid to ask or they're not sure they want to know—"What if it's bad?" If it's bad, believe me, you want to know. The more information you have on what the publishing house is doing behind the scenes, the better you'll be able to make good, smart decisions. Ask what the house is doing for promo, if they're buying co-op (front of store space for your book). See if you can get a copy of the sales catalog, which will tell you how you're being promoted in relationship to other titles. Once the book has been out a month or more, ask your agent to find out the chain store numbers.

Publish frequently. Not everyone can write a couple of books a year, but if you can—do it. In my opinion, many of the writers who have broken out in recent years have published frequently, many in back-to-back publishing programs. The more current titles you have, the more likely it will be that the bookstores will keep your backlist on the shelves. Certainly this is not the only road to the top, and you don't want to sacrifice quality for speed. But when it's time to pick deadlines and publishing schedules, try to optimize how often your books come out.

Whatever it takes—stay in the game. Even when things go wrong, publishing lines close, editors leave, numbers fall flat, books get poor reviews, and covers fail, don't give up on writing. New doors will open, but you have to have something to sell. Give yourself permission to be down for a day, and then get back up. Don't be afraid to write out of your comfort zone. Try a new niche. Your unique voice will go with you.

Trends come and go. About every seven years the publishing world changes. If you're lucky, your niche will never go out of style, but if it does, don't forget that a good book is still a good book. You might have to emphasize one part of a story over another to sell in a diminishing market, or elbow your way into another niche by writing across the genre. And hang on to the books that are suddenly out of fashion—before you know it, they'll be back in style.

Only compete with yourself. In publishing, there will always be people ahead of you and behind you. Wasting time on jealousy and envy will sap your creative energy.

Run your promotions—don't let them run you. Many authors get sucked into the competitive world of self-promotion. There's always a new bandwagon to jump on, whether it be bookmarks, video trailers, podcasts, blogs . . . do the promotions that make sense to you and don't try to keep up with everyone else. Some time ago I heard this great phrase: "A fabulous book is an author's triumph, and a bestselling book is a publisher's triumph." As an author, you can't control your book's destiny. There are too many factors that are beyond your control. Focus on the quality of the work, the promotions that support the publisher's efforts, but know that in most cases, it's the publisher's muscle and money that really make the big difference.

Enjoy the journey. At the end of the day, it's always about the book. Whether you're hitting each and every one of your goals, whether you're at the beginning or the middle of your career, it comes down to the tale you're spinning. Don't ever forget that your book will bring pleasure to someone else's life. You've created something valuable, something that came completely out of your imagination. That's a remarkable feat, and one very few people can accomplish. Take pride in the work. And don't ever give up. The only way to ensure failure is to quit. As long as you're writing, there's always a chance something incredible will come your way.

Barbara Freethy is a four-time RITA Award finalist and winner. She has written 26 books, many of which have been national bestsellers and have received numerous awards. Her most recent romantic suspense novels are *Silent Run* and *Silent Fall*, published in March/April 2008. For more information, visit her website at www.barbarafreethy.com.

Perseverance: The Writer's Journey
By Patricia Simpson

The Call to Adventure: That magic moment

Once, long ago, in a land far, far away, I was a fledgling writer—slaving away on my stories and losing myself in the world of imagination. I liked it there. I could control what people said and did. My characters held delicious conversations with each other. I could explore on paper what I could only dream of in real life—fantasies that included tall, dark, and handsome men who looked suspiciously like Pierce Brosnan. I wrote so much that the "e" fell off the striker key of my typewriter. But along the way, I learned the craft of writing a novel, and I sold to HarperMonogram in the early 1990s.

My world turned golden. Seeing my first book on the shelves was the most fulfilling day of my life. I won awards. I toyed with the concept of fame, of having an intimate conversation with Anne Rice instead of waiting in line for two hours to get her autograph. I dreamed of owning a Manhattan apartment, a townhouse in Charleston, maybe even a tropical tiki hut—each abode graced by a tall, dark, and handsome pool boy who looked remarkably like Pierce Brosnan.

The Sagging Middle: Show me the money!

Insert much typing here, a decade, thirteen published books, three publishing houses, a divorce, single parenthood, a full-time job, a career achievement award, a serious head injury, a lawsuit against HarperCollins, two and a half agents, and much more typing.

The Dark Moment: Fantasy versus reality check

Bank account	Dismal
Morale	Exhausted
Fame	Elusive
Awards	A slew
Dilemma	Keep killing myself pumping out two books a year with no social life (no life at all) or give writing a rest
Writing salary	25 cents an hour (if lucky)
Other job salary	50 dollars an hour (guaranteed)
Outcome	You do the math

I allowed myself a break, but I didn't stop writing. I wrote other things. I studied screenwriting. I studied high-concept theory, learned about plot paradigms, premise, and theme. During my lowest moments, I wondered if I could

135

still call myself a writer because I didn't see my name in print anywhere. I didn't pay quarterly taxes. Hardly anyone sent me fan letters. I even saw an article entitled "Whatever Happened To" — with my name on the list. That was a sad, sad day. But I never stopped thinking of myself as a writer.

The Resolution: Money is no object

After a hiatus, a second marriage, and moving to four cities in four years, I am seriously writing romantic fiction again. But in all the 'tween years, I never ceased to think of myself as a writer. It doesn't matter that I've sold only two books in the past four years. It wouldn't really matter if I weren't selling at all. I write because I'm a writer, not because I'm looking to become rich. At twenty-five cents an hour, you really have to love the work.

Selling doesn't define me as a writer. Writing defines me as a writer. I know in my heart that writing is something I will always do — that it's something I have to do, that it's something I am here to work at and perfect more than anything else in my life. If someone pays me a few thousand dollars for my trouble, fine. If not, fine. I am not about to quit writing! What would my characters do? Where would they go? What would I do with my constantly scheming mind?

Epilogue: The truth

You have to love writing to stick with it. The envelopes with the checks inside are just icing on the cake. But the bottom line is — and take it from a veteran — selling a book does not a writer make.

Award-winning paranormal author Patricia Simpson is hard at work on her fourteenth novel, *The Knight*, which features a medieval Scottish warrior resurrected by a woman on the brink of nervous breakdown. Patricia is known for creating stories with multiple levels and unusual characters, and has been hailed by reviewers as a premier writer of supernatural romance.

THE ULTIMATE RESOURCE FOR WRITING ROMANCE

Romance Writers of America

National Office
16000 Stuebner Airline Rd, Ste. 140
Spring, TX 77379
phone: 832.717.5200
fax: 832.717.5201
www.rwanational.org
info@rwanational.org

U.S. Chapters

Alabama
Gulf Coast Romance Writers: www.gccrwa.com
Heart of Dixie: www.heartofdixie.org
Southern Magic: www.southernmagic.org

Alaska
Alaska Romance Writers of America: www.akrwa.org

Arizona
Northern Arizona Romance Writers of America: www.narwa.com
Phoenix Desert Rose Chapter: www.desertroserwa.org
Saguaro Romance Writers (RWA-Tucson): www.tucsonrwa.org
Valley of the Sun Romance Writers: www.valleyofthesunrw.com

Arkansas
Diamond State Romance Authors: www.dsra-rwa.com

California
Black Diamond Romance Writers: www.bdrwa.com
East Valley Authors: www.eastvalleyauthors.com
Inland Valley Romance Writers: www.ivrwa.org
Los Angeles Romance Authors: www.lararwa.com
Monterey Bay Fiction Writers: www.baymoon.com/~mbc/
Orange County (California) Chapter: www.occrwa.org
RWA San Diego: www.rwasd.com
Sacramento Valley Rose: www.sacramentovalleyrose.com
San Francisco Area RWA: www.sfarwa.com
Silicon Valley RWA: www.svrwa.com
Wine Country Romance Writers: www.winecountryromancewriters.com

Colorado
Colorado Romance Writers: www.coloradoromancewriters.org
Heart of Denver Romance Writers: www.hodrw.com
Pikes Peak Romance Writes: www.pprw.org

Our authors give their Top Ten reasons to publish with
Samhain Publishing.

10. Samhain offers free, professional classes on everything
from promotion to bookkeeping.

9. The contracts are author-friendly & easy to understand.

8. The authors have cover art input with a professional
cover art staff.

7. Samhain is constantly expanding the company's
opportunities but not at the expense of company stability.

6. Excellent communication between staff and authors.

5. Monthly paychecks!

4. A supportive author group makes for a low-stress working
environment.

3. The staff works tirelessly to make sure each book is treated
like the ONLY book they publish.

2. Experienced editors work with authors to polish each book
like a gem.

1. Authors are always appreciated and welcomed!

Paperbacks are available at a bookstore near you. Electronic versions are available at:
www.samhainpublishing.com ○ www.mybookstoreandmore.com

Connecticut
Charter Oak Romance Writers: www.charteroakromancewriters.org
Connecticut Romance Writers (CTRWA): www.ctrwa.org
Romance Writers of Southern CT and Lower NY: www.romance-writers-colony.org

Delaware   No listings

Florida
Ancient City Romance Authors: http://web.mac.com/vickihinze/ACRA/Welcome.html
Central Florida Romance Writers: www.cfrwa.org
First Coast Romance Writers: www.firstcoastromancewriters.com
Florida Romance Writers: www.frwriters.org
Southwest Florida Romance Writers: www.swfrw.org
Space CoasT Authors of Romance (STAR): www.authorsofromance.com
Tampa Area Romance Authors (TARA): www.tararwa.com
Volusia County Romance Writers: www.vcrw.net

Georgia
Georgia Romance Writers: www.georgiaromancewriters.org
Heartland of Georgia Romance Writers: No website listed

Hawaii
Aloha Chapter: www.rwaaloha.org

Idaho
Coeur du Bois Chapter (Boise, ID): www.cbcrwa.com

Illinois
Chicago-North Romance Writers: www.chicagonorthrwa.org
Heart & Scroll RWA: www.heartandscroll.com
Love Designers Writers Club: www.rendezvousreviews.com
Prairie Hearts: www.geocities.com/prairiehearts
Quad Cities Romance Writers: No website listed
Windy City RWA: www.windycityrwa.com

Indiana
Indiana RWA: www.indianarwa.com
Northwest Indiana Romance Writers: www.nwinrwa.org

Iowa
Heart of Iowa Fiction Authors: www.hifarwa.org
Iowa Romance Novelists: www.iowaromancenovelists.org

Kansas
Mid-America Romance Authors (MARA): www.mararwa.com
Midwest Romance Writers: www.midwestromwriter.com
Wichita Area Romance Authors: www.warawriters.com

Kentucky
Kentucky Romance Writers: ww.kentuckyromancewriters.com
KYOWA: http://kyowaromance.tripod.com/
Louisville Romance Writers: www.louisvilleromancewriters.com

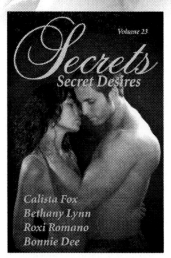

Louisiana
Coeur de Louisiane: www.cp-tel.net/dennisc/coeur.html
Heart of Louisiana (HeartLa): www.heartla.com
North Louisiana Storytellers and Authors of Romance (NOLA STARs): www.nolastars.com
SOLA (Southern Louisiana): www.solawriters.org

Maine
Maine Romance Writers of America: www.mainerwa.com

Maryland
Maryland Romance Writers: www.marylandromancewriters.org

Massachusetts
New England Chapter: www.necrwa.org

Michigan
Grand Rapids Region RWA: www.grrrwa.org
Greater Detroit RWA: www.gdrwa.org
Mid-Michigan RWA: http://midmichiganrwa.org

Minnesota
Northern Lights Writers: www.northernlightswriters.org
Midwest Fiction Writers (MFW): www.midwestfiction.com

Mississippi
Magnolia State Romance Writers: www.msrw.us

Missouri
Heartland Romance Authors (HeRA):
http://hera.romance-central.com
Mid-America Romance Authors (MARA): www.mararwa.com
Missouri Romance Writers of America (MoRWA): www.morwa.org

Montana   No listings

Nebraska
Cameo Romance Writers: www.cameoromancewriters.com
Nebraska Romance Writers: www.nebraskaromancewriters.com
Prairieland Romance Writers: www.prwne.com
Heartland Writers Group Omaha: www.heartlandwritersgroupomaha.com

Nevada
Cactus Rose Romance Writers: www.cactusroserwa.org

New Hampshire
New Hampshire Romance Writers of America: http://nhrwa.tripod.com

New Jersey
New Jersey Romance Writers: www.njromancewriters.org

New Mexico
Land of Enchantment Romance Authors (LERA): www.leranm.com

New York
Capital Region RWA: www.cr-rwa.org
Central New York Romance Writers: www.dm.net/~cnyrw/
Hudson Valley RWA: www.hvrwa.com
Lake Country Romance Writers: www.lcrw.org
Long Island Romance Writers: http://lirw.org
Romance Writers of Southern CT and Lower NY (CoLoNY): www.romance-writers-colony.org
RWA New York City: www.rwanyc.com
Saratoga Romance Writers of America: www.telltalepress.com/srwa.html
Southern Tier Authors of Romance: http://members.aol.com/STARRWA
Western New York Romance Writers: www.wnyrw.org

North Carolina
Carolina Romance Writers: www.carolinaromancewriters.com
Heart of Carolina Romance Writers: www.heartofcarolina.org

North Dakota   No listings

Ohio
Central Ohio Fiction Writers: www.cofw.org
KYOWA: kyowaromance.tripod.com
Maumee Valley RWA: www.mvrwa.net
Northeast Ohio Romance Writers of America (NEORWA): www.neorwa.com
Ohio Valley Romance Writers of America: www.ovrwa.com

Oklahoma
Oklahoma Romance Writers of America (OK-RWA): www.okrwa.com
Romance Writers Ink: www.rwi-rwa.com

Oregon
Mid-Willamette Valley RWA: www.midwillamettevalleyrwa.com
Rose City Romance Writers: www.rosecityromancewriters.com

Pennsylvania
Bucks County Romance Writers: www.buckscorw.org
Central Pennsylvania Romance Writers: www.cprw.org
Pocono/Lehigh Romance Writers: www.plrw.org
Valley Forge Romance Writers: www.vfrw.com
Western Pennsylvania Romance Writers: www.geocities.com/westernpa_romancewriters

Rhode Island   No listings

South Carolina
Lowcountry Romance Writers: www.lowcountryrwa.com

South Dakota   No listings

Tennessee
Music City Romance Writers: www.mcrw.com
River City Romance Writers: www.rivercityromancewriters.org
Smoky Mountain Romance Writers: www.smrw.org

Texas
Austin Chapter: www.austinrwa.com
Dallas Area Romance Authors (DARA): www.dallasromanceauthors.com
East Texas Chapter: www.easttexasrwa.com
Heart of Texas: www.geocities.com/hotrwa/
Houston Bay Area: www.hbarwa.com
North Texas Romance Writers of America: www.ntrwa.org
Northwest Houston RWA: www.northwesthoustonrwa.com
Red River Romance Writers: www.redriverromancewriters.com
San Antonio Romance Authors (SARA): www.sararwa.net
West Houston RWA: www.whrwa.com
Yellow Rose Romance Writers: www.yellowroserwa.com

Utah
Utah Romance Writers of America: www.utahrwa.com

Vermont   No Listings

Virginia
Chesapeake Romance Writers: www.crwrwa.org
Virginia Romance Writers: www.virginiaromancewriters.com

Washington
Eastside RWA: www.eastsiderwa.org
Greater Seattle Romance Writers of America: http://gsrwa.org/
Inland Empire Chapter: http://geocities.com/SoHo/Studios/2936/
Olympia Chapter: www.olympiarwa.org
Peninsula Romance Writers: www.penrwa.org

Washington, D.C.
Washington Romance Writers: www.wrwdc.com

West Virginia
KYOWA: http://kyowaromance.tripod.com/

Wisconsin
Wisconsin Romance Writers of America: www.wisrwa.org

Wyoming   No Listings

International Chapters
Calgary Association of RWA: www.calgaryrwa.com
Greater Vancouver Chapter: www.rwagvc.com
Marshlands Romance Writers: http://members.tripod.com/~MRW_RWA
Ottawa Romance Writers Association: www.ottawaromancewriters.com
Romance Writers of Atlantic Canada: www.romancewritersac.com
Toronto Romance Writers: www.torontoromancewriters.com
Vancouver Island Chapter: www.vicrwa.ca

Special-Interest Chapters

The Beau Monde (Regency): www.thebeaumonde.com
Celtic Hearts Romance Writers: www.celtichearts.org
Chick Lit Writers of the World: www.chicklitwriters.com
Electronic and Small Press Authors Network: www.espan-rwa.com
Elements of RWA (Non-traditional Romance Fiction): www.elementsofrwa.com
Faith, Hope, and Love, Inc.: www.faithhopelove-rwa.org
From the Heart Romance Writers: www.fthrw.com
Futuristic, Fantasy and Paranormal: www.romance-ffp.com
Golden Network Chapter (Golden Heart Contest Finalists and Winners): www.thegoldennetwork.com
Gothic Romance Writers, Inc.: www.gothrom.net
Hearts Through History Romance Writers: www.heartsthroughhistory.com
Mystery/Suspense Chapter (Kiss of Death): www.rwamysterysuspense.org
Outreach International Romance Writers: www.oirw.net
Passionate Ink (Erotic Romance): www.passionateink.org
Published Authors Special Interest Chapter/PASIC: www.pasic.net
Heartbeat RWA (Medical Romance): www.heartbeatrwa.com
RWA Online: www.rwaonlinechapter.org
Scriptscene: www.scriptscene.org

Please read and follow submission guidelines before contacting publishers or agents. Additionally, double-check all contact information. Editors and agents change houses, go out of business, etc. While every effort has been made to insure the accuracy of this information, please verify all of it before contact any agent or publisher. This information is for informational purposes only and readers with questions should consult the appropriate legal and accounting authorities.

LITERARY AGENTS SELLING ROMANCE

3 Seas Literary Agency
Michelle Grajkowski
queries@threeseaslit.com
www.threeseaslit.com

T (608) 467-8045

AEI Literary Management
Ken Atchity
c/o AEI Submissions
www.aeionline.com

518 S. Fairfax Avenue
Los Angeles CA 90036
T (323) 932 0407

The Agency Group
Caroline Greeven
CarolineGreeven@theagencygroup.com
Marc Gerald
marcgerald@theagencygroup.com
www.theagencygroup.com

1880 Century Park East, Suite 711
Los Angeles, CA 90067
T (310) 385-2800 | F (310) 385-1220

Alive Communications, Inc.
Beth Jusino
www.alivecom.com

7680 Goddard Street, Suite 200
Colorado Springs, CO 80920
T (719) 260-7080

AMB Literary Management
Amy Moore-Benson
ambliterarymanagement@rogers.com
CANADA

104 Fulton Avenue
Toronto, ON M4K 1X8
T (416) 467-1695

The Axelrod Agency
Steve Axelrod
steve@axelrodagency.com
axelrodagency.com

55 Main Street
P.O. Box 357
Chatham, NY 12037
T (518) 392-2100 | F (518) 392-2944

Barrett Books
Audra Barrett
www.barrettbooksagency.com

12138 Central Avenue, Suite 183
Mitchellville, MD 20721

Blake Friedmann Literary, Film & TV Agency
Carole Blake
The Submissions Department
Blake Friedmann Literary Agency
www.blakefriedmann.co.uk

122 Arlington Road, Second Floor
London NW1 7HP
ENGLAND
T (020) 7284 0408 | F (020) 7284 0442

Bleecker Street Associates
Agnes Birnbaum
New York, NY 10012

532 LaGuardia Place #617

BookEnds, LLC
Jessica Faust
JFaust@bookends-inc.com
Kim Lionetti
KLionetti@bookends-inc.com
www.bookends-inc.com

136 Long Hill Road
Gillette, NJ 07933

Bradford Literary Agency
Laura Bradford
laura@bradfordlit.com
www.bradfordlit.com

5694 Mission Center Road # 347
San Diego, CA 92108

Brown Literary Agency
Roberta Brown
broagent@aol.com
www.brownliteraryagency.com

410 7th Street NW
Naples, FL 34120-2039

Caren Johnson Literary Agency
cjla.squarespace.com/send-email
cjla.squarespace.com/welcome

The Cooke Agency, Vancouver Office
reception@thehardingagency.com
www.thehardingagency.com
V6E 4T2 CANADA
T (604) 331-9330 | F (604) 331-9328

P.O. Box 76003
Vancouver, BC

The Cooke Agency, Toronto Office
agents@cookeagency.ca
www.cookeagency.ca
M4W 3M4 CANADA
T (416) 406-3390 | F (416) 406-3389

278 Bloor St. East, Suite 305
Toronto, ON

Crichton & Associates
Sha-Shana Crichton
cricht1@aol.com
www.crichton-associates.com

6940 Carroll Avenue
Takoma Park, MD 20912
T (301) 495-9663 | F (202) 318-0050

Curtis Brown Group Ltd.
Haymarket House
cb@curtisbrown.co.uk
www.curtisbrown.co.uk
T (020) 7393 4400 | F (020) 7393 4401

28 - 29 Haymarket
London SW1Y 4SP
ENGLAND

Denise Marcil Literary Agency
Maura Kye-Casella
www.denisemarcilagency.com

156 Fifth Avenue, Suite 625
New York, NY 10010-7002

Donald Maass Literary Agency
Jennifer Jackson
info@maassagency.com
www.maassagency.com

121 West 27th Street, Suite 801
New York, NY 10001
T (212) 727-8383 | F (212) 727-3271

the All About Us series by Shelley Adina

It's All About Us (May 2008)

Lissa Mansfield is used to being in the "in" crowd--but being accepted by the popular girls at posh Spencer Academy boarding school in San Francisco is a lot harder than she thought. And then there's her loudmouth roommate, Gillian Chang, who's not just happy to be a Christian herself--she's determined to out Lissa, too. If Lissa can just keep her faith under wraps long enough to hook Callum McCloud, the hottest guy in school, she'll be golden. But when Callum pressures her to go all the way with him, Lissa has to decide how far is too far. Between that and shopping for a knockout dress and booking the hottest celeb for the Benefactor's Day Ball ... who knew finding a place at Spencer Academy would be so complicated?

The Fruit of my Lipstick (August 2008)

Gillian Chang starts her second term at Spencer Academy prepared to focus on her studies, her faith, and her friends. She plays a dozen musical instruments and can recite the periodic table of the elements backward. She's totally prepared for everything--except love! She's falling hard for Lucas Hayes, but she never seems to be able to measure up and be the girlfriend he wants. He's under a lot of pressure to achieve--maybe that's why he's short-tempered sometimes. With her heart on the line, Gillian conceals more and more from her friends. So when she's accused of selling exam answer sheets, even her girlfriends, Lissa Mansfield and Carly Aragon, wonder if it can be true. Gillian will need the power of honesty--with herself and with Lucas--to show what she's really made of.

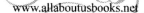
www.allaboutusbooks.net

Shelley Adina wrote her first teen novel when she was 13. It was rejected by the literary publisher to whom she sent it, but he did say she knew how to tell a story. That was enough to keep her going through the rest of her adolescence, a career, a move to another country, a B.A. in Literature, an M.A. in Writing Popular Fiction, and countless manuscript pages. Shelley is a world traveler and pop culture junkie with an incurable addiction to designer handbags. She loves writing about fun and faith--with a side of glamour.

God, girlfriends, and a great handbag. What else do you need to survive high school?

Elaine P. English, PLLC
Attorney & Literary Agent
ElaineEngl@aol.com
www.elaineenglish.com

4710 41st Street, NW, Suite D
Washington, DC 20016
T (202) 362-5190 | F (202) 362-5192

Elaine Koster Agency
Elaine Koster
elainekost@aol.com

55 Central Park West, Suite #6
New York, NY 10023
T (212) 362-9488 | F (212) 712-0164

Essential Works
Mal Peachey
info@essentialworks.co.uk
essentialworks.co.uk

168a Camden Street
London NW1 9PT
ENGLAND
T (020) 7485 1341 | F (020) 7267 1119

Ethan Ellenberg
agent@ethanellenberg.com
www.ethanellenberg.com

548 Broadway #5E
New York, NY 10012
T (212) 431-4554 | F (212) 941-4652

Evan Marshall Agency
evanmarshall@thenovelist.com
www.thenovelist.com

Six Tristam Place
Pine Brook, NJ 07058-9445

Ferguson Literary Agency
Cheryl Ferguson
Submissions@fergusonliteraryagency.com
www.fergusonliteraryagency.com

Fletcher & Parry
Melissa Chinchillo
www.fletcherparry.com

78 Fifth Avenue, Third Floor
New York, NY 10011

Frances Goldin Literary Agency
Ellen Geiger
eg@goldinlit.com
www.goldinlit.com

57 E. 11th Street, Suite 5B
New York, NY 10003
T (212) 777-0047

Gelfman Schneider
Deborah Schneider

250 W 57TH Street, Suite 2515
New York, NY 10107-2595
T (212) 245-1993

The Gernert Company
Stephanie Cabot
info@thegernertco.com
www.thegernertco.com

136 East 57th Street, 18th Floor
New York, NY 10022

Hartline Literary Agency
Tamela Hancock Murray
tamela@hartlineliterary.com
www.hartlineliterary.com

123 Queenston Drive
Pittsburgh, PA 15235
T (412) 829-2483

Harvey Klinger
Andrea Somberg
queries@harveyklinger.com
harveyklinger.com

300 West 55th Street, Suite 11V
New York, NY 10019

Hopkins Literary Associates
Pam Hopkins
phopkin1@rochester.rr.com

ICM
International Creative Management
Tina Wexler (NY office)
twexler@icmtalent.com
www.icmtalent.com

825 Eighth Avenue
New York, NY 10019
T (212) 556-5600

Imprint Agency
Stephany Evans
imprintagency@earthlink.net
www.imprintagency.com

240 West 35th Street, Suite 500
New York, NY 10001

Inkwell Management
Alexis Hurley
info@inkwellmanagement.com
www.inkwellmanagement.com

521 Fifth Avenue, 26th Floor
New York, NY 10175
T (212) 922-3500 | F (212) 922-0535

International Scripts
H.P. Tanner

1a Kidbrooke Park Road
London SE3 0LR
ENGLAND
T (020) 8319 8666 | F (020) 8319 0801

Irene Goodman Literary Agency
Barbara Poelle
queries@irenegoodman.com
www.irenegoodman.com

80 Fifth Avenue, Suite 1101
New York, NY 10011
T (212) 604-0330 | F (212) 675-1381

JET Literary Associates, Inc.
Elizabeth Trupin-Pulli
etp@jetliterary.com
www.jetliterary.com

2570 Camino San Patricio
Santa Fe, NM 87505
T (505) 474-9139

The Knight Agency, Inc.
Nephele Tempest
Pamela Harty
submissions@knightagency.net

All submissions are to be made
electronically.
www.knightagency.net

Larsen/Pomada Literary Agency
Laurie McLean
laurie@agentsavant.com

P.O. Box 258
La Honda, CA 94020

Larsen/Pomada Literary Agency
www.larsen-pomada.com

1029 Jones St.
San Francisco, CA 94109
T (415) 673-0939

Laura Langlie Agency
laura@lauralanglie.com

239 Carroll Street
Brooklyn, NY 11231
T (718) 855-8102 | F (718) 855-4450

Levine Greenberg Literary Agency, Inc.
Stephanie Kip Rostan
srostan@levinegreenberg.com
James Levine
jlevine@levinegreenberg.com
www.levinegreenberg.com

307 Seventh Avenue, Suite 2407
New York, NY 10001
T (212) 337-0934 | F (212) 337-0948

Liza Dawson Associates
queryliza@LizaDawsonAssociates.com
www.lizadawsonassociates.com
T (212) 465-9071 | F (212) 947-0460

350 Seventh Avenue, Suite 2003
New York, NY 10001

MacGregor Literary
Chip MacGregor
Solicited queries only
submissions@macgregorliterary.com
macgregorliterary.com

2373 N.W. 185th Avenue, Suite 165
Hillsboro, OR 97124-7076

Mortimer Literary Agency
Kelly Mortimer
Solicited submissions only
query@mortimerliterary.com
www.mortimerliterary.com

52645 Paui Road
Aguanga, CA 92536
T (951) 763-2600

Natasha Kern Literary Agency
Natasha Kern
queries@natashakern.com
www.natashakern.com

P. O. Box 1069
White Salmon, WA 98672

Nelson Literary Agency, LLC
Kristin Nelson
query@nelsonagency.com
www.nelsonagency.com
Please, no phone/snail mail queries

1732 Wazee Street, Suite 207
Denver, CO 80202
T 303.292.2805

Paul S. Levine Literary Agency
Paul Levine
pslevine@ix.netcom.com
home.netcom.com/~pslevine/lawliterary.html

1054 Superba Avenue
Venice, CA 90291-3940
T (310) 450-6711 | F (310) 450-0181

Pavilion Literary Management
Jeff Kellogg, President
jeff@pavilionliterary.com
www.pavilionliterary.com

660 Massachusetts Avenue, Suite 4
Boston, MA 02118
T. (617) 792-5218

Prospect Agency
Emily Sylvan Kim
Attn: Submissions
www.prospectagency.com

285 Fifth Avenue, PMB 445
Brooklyn, NY 11215
T (718) 788-3217 | F (718) 360-9582

Richard Curtis Associates, Inc.
rcurtis@curtisagency.com
www.curtisagency.com

171 East 74th Street, Floor 2
New York, NY 10021

Richard Henshaw Group (World)
Susannah Taylor
Devi.Pillai@hbgusa.com

22 West 23rd Street, 5th Floor
New York, NY 10010
T (212) 414-1172 | F (212) 414-1182

Rosenberg Group
Barbara Collins Rosenberg
www.rosenberggroup.com
No Inspirational, Time Travel, Futuristic or Paranormal

23 Lincoln Avenue
Marblehead, MA 01945

Sandra Dijkstra Literary Agency World
Kevan Lyon
kevan@dijkstraagency.com
sdla@dijkstraagency.com

1155 Camino Del Mar
PMB 515
Del Mar, CA 92104-2605
T (858) 755-3115 | F (858) 792-2822

Spectrum Literary Agency
Lucienne Diver
www.spectrumliteraryagency.com

P.O. Box 2659
Land O Lakes, FL 34639
T (212) 362-4323 | F (212) 362-4562

The Steve Laube Agency
Christian Literature
www.stevelaube.com

5025 N. Central Avenue, #635
Phoenix, AZ 85012-1502
T (602) 336-8910 | F (602) 532-7123

The Stuart Agency
Andrew Stuart
andrew@stuartagency.com

260 W. 52 Street #24C
New York, NY 10019
T (212) 586-2711 | F (212) 977-1488

Talbot Fortune Agency (NA)
Gail Fortune
gailfortune@talbotfortuneagency.com
queries@talbotfortuneagency.com
www.talbotfortuneagency.com

Trident Media Group
Kimberly Whalen
T (212) 333-1505
whalen.assistant@tridentmediagroup.com
Jenny Bent
jbent@tridentmediagroup.com
Robert Gottlieb
gottlieb.assistant@tridentmediagroup.com
www.tridentmediagroup.com

41 Madison Avenue, 36th Fl.
New York, NY 10010
T (212) 262-4810 | F (212) 262-4849

T (212) 333-1535

T (212) 333-1500

Vivian Beck Agency
Vivian Beck
Query@vivianbeck.com; Vivian.Beck@vivianbeck.com; www.vivianbeck.com

Wade & Doherty Literary Agency
Principal: Robin Wade
rw@rwla.com
Partner: Ms Broo Doherty
bd@rwla.com
www.rwla.com

33 Cormorant Lodge
Thomas More Street
London E1W 1AU
ENGLAND
T (020) 7488 4171 | F 020 7488 4172

Wendy Sherman Associates
www.wsherman.com

450 Seventh Avenue, Suite 2307
New York, NY 10123
T (212) 279-9027 | F (212) 279-8863

Writers House
Robin Rue
www.writershouse.com

21 West 26th Street
New York, NY 10010

Wylie-Merrick Literary Agency
Sharene Martin
sharenembrown@wylie-merrick.com.
smartin@wylie-merrick.com
www.wylie-merrick.com

PUBLISHERS SELLING ROMANCE

Avon
Carrie Feron
Lucia Macro
Lyssa Keusch
May Chen
Gena Pearson
avonceromance@harpercollins.com.
www.avonbooks.com

10 East 53rd Street
New York, NY 10022
T (212) 207-7250 | F (212) 207-6998

Ballantine Books
Linda Marrow
Melody Guy
www.randomhouse.com/rhpg/

Random House, Inc.
1540 Broadway
New York, NY 10036

Bantam Dell
Caitlin Alexander
Shauna Summers
Kate Miciak
www.randomhouse.com

1540 Broadway
New York, NY 10036
T (212) 782-9000 | F (212) 302-7985

Berkley
Cindy Hwang – Berkley
Leis Pederson – Berkley Sensation
Kate Seaver – Berkley Sensation
www.penguinputnam.com

375 Hudson Street
New York, NY 10014
T (212) 366-2000 | F (212) 366-2385

Bethany House Publishers
David Long
www.bethanyhouse.com

11400 Hampshire Avenue S
Minneapolis, MN 55438
F (952) 996-1304

Dorchester Publishing
Chris Keeslar
Leah Hultenschmidt
dorchpub@dorchesterpub.com
admin@smoochya.com
www.dorchesterpub.com

200 Madison Avenue #2000
New York, NY 10016

Dutton
Julie Doughty
www.penguinputnam.com

375 Hudson Street
New York, NY 10014
T (212) 366-2000 I F (212) 366-3393

Echelon Press Publishing
Karen Syed
Admin@echelonpress.com

9735 Country Meadows Lane 1-D
Laurel, MD 20723
T (410) 878-7113 I F (410) 988-2864

Ellora's Cave/Cerridwen
E-Publisher
Submissions@ellorascave.com
www.ellorascave.com

Grand Central Publishing (formerly Warner Books)
Karen Thomas
Caryn Karmatz-Rudy
Rebecca Isenberg
Devi Pillai
www.hachettebookgroupusa.com

237 Park Avenue
New York, NY 10017
T (212) 364-1200 I F (212) 364-0928

iUniverse, Inc.
Harlem Writers Guild Press/Publishing Services
Bloomington, IN 47403
www.iuniverse.com/packages/specialty/hwg-press.htm

1663 Liberty Drive, Suite 300

Harlequin Books, MIRA Books
225 Duncan Mill Road
Don Mills, ON
M3B 3K9 CANADA
Harlequin Books, Silhouette Books
Steeple Hill Books
233 Broadway, Suite 1001
New York, NY 10279
T (212) 553-4200
Harlequin Mills & Boon Ltd.
Eton House, 18-24 Paradise Road
Richmond, Surrey, United Kingdom
TW9 1SR
www.eharlequin.com/articlepage.html?articleId=538&chapter=0
Harvest House
LaRae Weikert
Kim Moore
www.harvesthousepublishers.com/about_manuscript.cfm

Headline Little Black Dress
Catherine Cobain   United Kingdom
Mary-Anne Harrington
mary-anne.harrington@headline.co.uk.
www.headline.co.uk.

Juno
Paula Guran
editor@juno-books.com
www.juno-books.com/guidelines.html

Kensington Publishing
Kate Duffy - Kensington   830 Third Avenue, 16th Floor
Danielle Chiotti - Kensington   New York NY 10022-6222
John Scognamiglio – Kensington, Aphrodisia   T (212) 407-1500 | F (212) 935-0699
Karen Thomas - Dafina
www.kensingtonbooks.com.

Linden Bay Romance, LLC
Stephanie Wardwell-Gaw   3529 Greenglen Circle
Nicole Bunting   Palm Harbor, Florida 34684
www.lindenbayromance.com/submissions.html

LooseID
submissions@loose-id.com
www.loose-id.com/prospective.aspx

Multnomah Publishers
Kevin Marks   204 W Adams Avenue
Rod Morris   P O Box 1720
www.multnomahbooks.com   Sisters, OR 97759
                                     T (541) 549-1144 | F (541) 549-2044

Waterbrook Press
Dudley Delffs   Random House
www.randomhouse.com   2375 Telstar Drive #160
Colorado Springs, CO 80920   T (719) 590-4999 | F (719) 590-8977

NAL (New American Library)
Kara Welsh   375 Hudson Street
Laura Cifelli   New York, NY 10014
Tracy Bernstein   T (212) 366-2000 | F (212) 366-2385
www.penguinputnam.com

Plume
www.penguinputnam.com   375 Hudson Street
                                     New York, NY 10014
                                     T (212) 366-2000 | F (212) 366-2385

Pocket Books
Micki Nuding   1230 Avenue of the Americas
Lauren McKenna   New York NY 10020-1513
www.simonandschuster.com   www.simonsays.com

Putnam
www.penguinputnam.com

375 Hudson Street
New York, NY 10014
T (212) 366-2000 | F (212) 366-3393

Revell/Baker Books
Lonnie Hull DuPont
bakerpublishinggroup.com

PO Box 6287
Grand Rapids, MI 49516-6287
T (800) 877-2665 | F (800) 398-3111

Seventh Window Publications
Ken Harrison
guidelines@seventhwindow.com
www.seventhwindow.com

P.O. Box 603165
Providence, RI 02906-0165

Shaye Areheart Books
Shaye Areheart
www.randomhouse.com
www.randomhouse.com/crown/shaye

1540 Broadway
New York, NY 10036
T (212) 782-9000 | F (212) 302-7985

Sourcebooks, Inc.
Deb Werksman
deb.werksman@sourcebooks.com
www.sourcebooks.com/content/authors_romance_submission_guidelines.asp

955 Connecticut Avenue #5310
Bridgeport, CT 06607

St. Martin's Press
Monique Patterson
Rose Hilliard
Jennifer Weis
christina.harcar@stmartins.com

175 Fifth Avenue
New York NY 10010
T (212) 674-5151
www.stmartins.com

Tekno Books
John Helfers
tekno@new.rr.com

P.O. Box 8296
Green Bay, WI 54308

Thomas Dunne Books
Diana Szu

St. Martin's Press
175 Fifth Avenue
New York NY 10010

Tom Doherty Associates, LLC
Paranormal Romance, Acquisitions editor
www.tor-forge.com/Faq.aspx

175 Fifth Avenue
New York, NY 10010
T (212) 388-0100

Featured Authors

JOANN SMITH
AINSWORTH   Author of novels relating that
courage makes ordinary people extraordinary ™

When I carried wood as a pre-teen so my Great Aunt Martha could stoke up the iron stove to prepare dinner, I wasn't thinking, "I could use this in a novel someday." Yet almost sixty years later, the skills I learned from my horse-and-buggy ancestors translate into a backdrop for my novels.

Samhain Publishing, Ltd. e-pub release June 2008.

OUT OF THE DARK -- A blind Anglo-Saxon gentlewoman fears vengeance when she overhears a conspiracy plot. The Norman sheriff is torn between his heart and family loyalty when he falls in love with this Saxon beauty while rooting out corruption that may implicate his half brother.

Blinded---she by nature, he by loyalty
(a medieval romance with a touch of paranormal and a lot of suspense)

I completed five novels (2 medieval and 2 western historical romances and a paranormal suspense).

To learn more, visit **www.joannsmithainsworth.com**.

Allison Brennan New York Times Bestselling Author

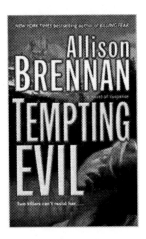

Book Two in the
Prison Break Trilogy
on sale now!

Haunted by the loss of her husband and child, Joanna Sutton has found refuge at her family's secluded lodge. But her haven soon becomes a hell. During the ferocious blizzard, a local Boy Scout troop is stranded in the wilderness, compelling Jo to spearhead a desperate rescue mission, aided by a newly arrived stranger with an unknown agenda.

Meanwhile, Sheriff Tyler McBride hears that two escaped convicts are fast approaching Big Sky Country. Hoping to warn Jo, he faxes over the men's mug shots. But they never reach their intended recipient. Then Tyler makes a shocking discovery: two people are dead, and a killer is among the group, along with the woman Tyler loves, searching for his lost son.

More than one innocent life is at stake. For the sake of those Jo cares about most, and for her own survival, she'll need all the cunning, courage, and passion she can muster to survive the mounting terror.

New York Times bestselling author and three-time RITA ® finalist Allison Brennan is the author of eight romantic thrillers.

Published in eight languages and in the UK, Allison has also won the Reviewers Choice Award from *Romantic Times* for Best Suspense of 2006 (THE KILL) and is a 2007 nominee for Best Contemporary Mystery (SEE NO EVIL).

Don't miss the first and last books of the Prison Break trilogy:
KILLING FEAR (on sale now) and PLAYING DEAD (9/30/08).

**Stop by and visit Allison on the web,
at http://www.AllisonBrennan.com**

Dianna Love

The Dark Edge of Romantic Suspense

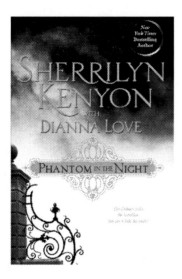

Terri Mitchell is working undercover for the Bureau of American Defense, investigating a drug kingpin of funding terrorism. When bizarre rumors begin to surface of a ghost terrorizing members of that ring, she becomes suspicious, but doesn't believe in the paranormal. An eerie encounter with someone in the dark leaves her shaken. Is this phantom really a spirit conjured up from the depth of the bayou, or a man set on a course of vengeance?

Now two people on opposite sides of the law with no reason to trust each other must join forces or die.
And if they die, a deadly attack will be unleashed on thousands of innocent people.

*Dianna co-wrote this book with #1 NYT best seller Sherrilyn Kenyon

Dianna Love (RITA Award winner as Dianna Love Snell) writes contemporary and paranormal romantic suspense. When not researching her next action-adventure story she presents national workshops on multiple subjects. Dianna and Mary Buckham's highly successful Plot Your Book In 2 Days Retreats will be published as part of a 2009 Break Into Fiction™: Simple Steps to Complex Novels book. (www.BreakIntoFiction.com)

Watch for Dianna's debut paranormal novella –
MIDNIGHT KISS GOODBYE
(St. Martin's Press anthology DEAD AFTER DARK – September 2008)

Stop by and visit Dianna on the web, at
http://www.AuthorDiannaLove.com

Margaret Lucke - Love, Ghosts and Murder

"A suspenseful, intriguing first entry in an innovative new series. Margaret Lucke is an exceptional writer."
— Bestselling mystery author Marcia Muller

"Margaret Lucke has found a new twist on haunted houses, as well as presenting an intriguing mystery mixed with romance."
— Bestselling fantasy author Chelsea Quinn Yarbro

Margaret Lucke is proud to join the ranks of romance writers with *House of Whispers*, in which real estate agent Claire Scanlan finds love and danger when she tries to sell a home that's haunted by the victims of a murder. It's the first in her Supernatural Properties series from Juno Books. Look for the second, *Mansion of Desire*, in 2009. Margaret's earlier novel, *A Relative Stranger*, was an Anthony Award nominee for Best First Mystery, and she has also written two how-to books about the craft of writing.

Stop by and visit Margaret on the web, at http://www.margaretlucke.com

Carolina Montague

The Tennessee Tussle

Jesse Murdoch is a preacher with the gift to heal, but whenever he uses his gift it carries a heavy price. There is no way he can let his parishioners know what he must do when he exercises his gift.

Laney Parker is a devout Christian with the gift of music, but in order to support her daughter she has to use her gift to play bluegrass in a band with barely a stitch of clothing. No way can she let the gorgeous Pastor Murdoch know what she does for a living. Worlds collide when Jesse decides to date Laney. When a producer from ROCK TV discovers the Tennessee Tussle Band, the jig is up.

Author of Door in the Sky
http://www.carolinamontague.com

Go ahead—pick up that deck of golden tarot cards.

You know you want to. They're calling to you. They're beautiful.

Turn over the card that comes to your hand, the card that will change your life forever...

You've just entered the world of...

THE FORBIDDEN TAROT

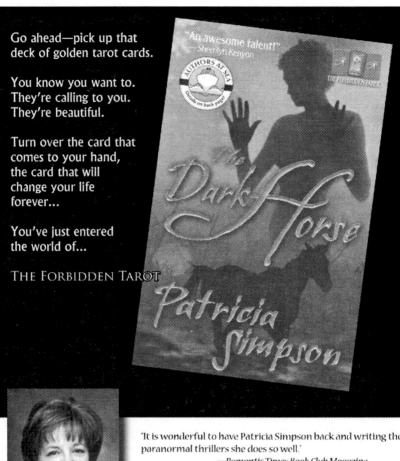

"It is wonderful to have Patricia Simpson back and writing the paranormal thrillers she does so well."
—*Romantic Times Book Club Magazine*

"Patricia Simpson has created a series that will surely entertain readers for a long time to come."
—*Coffee Time Romance*

"Unique, interesting, exciting, and just plain fun."
—*The Romance Reader's Connection*

Find book details and fabulous writing tips & tricks at:
www.patriciasimpson.com

Earlier titles now available as Kindle Books at Amazon.com.

She hates him for capturing her, even as her traitorous body surrenders to his masterful touch . . . .

KARIN TABKE

The sensual historical romance from the author of *Skin* and *Good Girl Gone Bad*

MASTER
of
SURRENDER

The Blood Sword Legacy Begins

Karin Tabke

Hot Cops, and Hot Knights

"Karin Tabke's *Good Girl Gone Bad, Skin,* "Redemption" in *What You Can't See,* and *Jaded* have won accolades and left her readers panting for more!

"Tabke masterfully creates sexual tension . . ." Romantic Times.

"Karin Tabke-an exciting new voice in contemporary erotica-turns up the heat with her sizzling debut..." —Powell's Books

"Redemption offers up a less than perfect hero readers are sure to find fascinating. With deft narrative, edgy dialogue and a unique story, Redemption is a sure winner." —Romance Reviews Today

The Blood Sword Legacy
Begins!

Bound by a brotherhood forged in the hell of a Saracen prison, eight Blood Swords – mercenary knights for William the Conqueror – set out to claim their legacies the only way they can: by right of arms, by right of victory, by right of conquest.

In bookstores June 24, 2008

Stop by and visit Karin on the web, at
http://www.karintabke.com

Tawny Weber

Hot, Sassy Romance

"**Double Dare** establishes
Tawny Weber as a new force
in the Blaze lineup"
—5 Stars, CataRomance.

"**Double Dare** mixes sizzling
sex, strong characters and
suspense into an exciting,
satisfying book."
—4 Stars, Romantic Times

"**Does She Dare** is an excellent read filled with steamy sex scenes that don't
overpower the eomotional connection between the characters."—5 Angels,
Fallen Angels Reviews

"**Does She Dare** is another sinfully spicy and chocolate sweet read by the
highly entertaining and creative Tawny Weber." —Romance Junkies

Tawny Weber is usually found
dreaming up stories in her California
home, surrounded by dogs, cats
and kids.

 A three-time Golden Heart finalist,
when Tawny's not writing hot, spicy
stories for Blaze, she's shopping for the
perfect pair of boots or drooling over
Johnny Depp pictures (when her
husband isn't looking, of course).

Her September Blaze, RISQUÉ
BUSINESS will be followed by back-to-
back Blaze's in Spring 2009 – be sure
to check them out!

**Stop by and visit Tawny on the web, at
http://www.tawnyweber.com**

It's All About the Sexy Attitude